FROM
ROUND TABLE
TO
GRAIL CASTLE

ISABEL WYATT

END PAPERS AND DUST JACKET:
Tapestries designed by Edward Burne-Jones and woven by William Morris & Company. By courtesy of Birmingham Museum & Art Gallery.
Front: Arming and Departure of the Knights
Back: The Holy Grail

Acknowledgments are due to The Golden Blade 1969 for permission to use "The Woodward of Broceliande".
Verlag Urachhaus for permission to quote from "Der Gral und seine Hüter" by Rudolf Meyer.
Rudolf Steiner Nachlassverwaltung for permission to quote from lectures by Rudolf Steiner.
University of Washington Press for a short quotation from Professor Skeel's "Romance of Perceval in Prose".
J. M. Dent & Sons Ltd, from material from the Everyman series in which have appeared many of the collections of legends cited in this book.

LAYOUT: Arne Klingborg

Printed by Affordable Print Ltd, Cornwall

The Lanthorn Press acknowledges most gratefully the grant given by the Cotswold Chine School for this production of *From Round Table to Grail Castle*.

ISBN 0 906155 09 6

FROM
ROUND TABLE
TO
GRAIL CASTLE

ISABEL WYATT

the lanthorn press

"The Stories of Arthur
are
The Acts of the Giant Albion"

William Blake

FROM ROUND TABLE TO GRAIL CASTLE

The Arthur Stream and the Grail Stream
TWELVE STUDIES IN ARTHURIAN AND
GRAIL LITERATURE IN THE LIGHT OF
ANTHROPOSOPHY

by
ISABEL WYATT
with an introduction by
JOAN RUDEL

The variants Grail – Graal; Guinevere – Guinievre – Guenever; Lancelot – Launcelot; Parsifal – Parzival – Perceval – Percivale; Sangreal – Sancgreal have been used in accordance with the sources quoted. Arthur is to be taken as a title given to successive initiates of the Arthur Mysteries, indicating that the same supersensible being was working behind and through them all.

CONTENTS

INTRODUCTION

Towards the end of the 12th century Alanus ab Insulis, that renowned teacher in the School of Chartres, spoke of King Arthur in a way that was at the same time valid for his own era and a prophecy for centuries to come. He said, "What place is there within the bounds of the empire of Christendom to which the winged praise of Arthur the Briton has not extended? Who is there, I ask, who does not speak of Arthur the Briton, since he is but little less known to the peoples of Asia than to the Britons, as we are informed by pilgrims who return from Eastern lands? The peoples of the East speak of him as do those of the West, though separated by the breadth of the whole world."

This was written three hundred years before Sir Thomas Malory finished composing his Morte d'Arthur, still the most-used source-book of these stories in English, and eight hundred years before Edward Burne-Jones and William Morris, their imaginations fired by the Arthurian exploits, created the beautiful tapestries reproduced in this book.

Despite the continuing efforts of scholars and historians there is, however, no documentary proof of the existence of a historical King Arthur. Nor can anyone point with certainty to the physical whereabouts of Camelot or Avalon or Carbonek, or that mysterious lake from whose waters arose the sword Excalibur. Yet throughout the centuries and right on into our own times peasants and kings, saints and warriors, painters and sculptors, poets and musicians have found inspiration in these stories of the deeds of King Arthur and his Knights and the interwoven theme of the Grail.

How can we account for the continuing and widespread interest in these legends? The answer to this question may have to be sought in a world other than in the physical world of time and space that man inhabits between birth and death. These stories have maintained their perennial appeal because they speak to the hidden depths of the human heart. They answer its longing for a world that does not partake of the transitory nature of our earthly environment, a world of eternally-existing realities. The language of legend reveals the truths of this other world in great imaginative pictures. In the twelve studies of this book the author attempts to penetrate to the spiritual realities behind the happenings in the various versions of the Arthurian and Grail stories, as they are affirmed and illumined by Rudolf Steiner's spiritual-scientific researches.

JOAN RUDEL

CHAPTER I

THE WOODWARD OF BROCELIANDE

In 1891 a Danish peat-bog yielded up, in sections, a magnificent silver cauldron of Celtic workmanship of the second or first century B.C. – the now famous Gundestrup Bowl. Not only is it unique in size and weight (42 centimetres in height, 69 centimetres in diameter, nearly 9 kilograms in weight), but the repoussé scenes which adorn it both without and within place it among the great masterpieces of Celtic art.

One such panel on its inner face portrays the Celtic god Cernussos in his role of Lord of the Animals, elegant antlers on his heads, his cultic stag beside him, antelope, boar, dolphin and other creatures standing or sporting about him.

This woodland scene calls to mind, by its very mingling of correspondences and contrasts, that other woodland scene described in the Welsh mabinogi, *The Lady of the Fountain*, when the Arthurian knight Sir Kynon tells his companions, Sir Owain and Sir Kay, how he was directed to the magic fountain of the title:

"Within the wood thou wilt come to a sheltered glade with a mound in the centre. And thou wilt see a black man of great stature on the top of the mound. He is not smaller in size than two of the men of this world. He has but one foot; and one eye in the middle of his forehead. And he has a club of iron, and there are no two men in the world who would not find their burden in that club. He is not a comely man, but on the contrary he is exceedingly ill-favoured; and he is the woodward of that wood. And thou wilt see a thousand wild animals grazing around him. Enquire of him that way."

Sir Kynon relates how, when he did indeed come to this black giant, he asked him "what power he held over those animals." "I will show thee, little man," said he. "And took his club in his hand, and with it he struck a stag a great blow, so that he brayed vehemently, and at his braying the animals came together, as numerous as the stars in the sky. There were serpents and dragons and divers sorts of animals. And he looked at them and bade them go and feed; and they bowed their heads and did him homage as vassals to their lord. Then I enquired of him the way, and he became very rough in his manner to me."

Fired by Sir Kynon's story, Sir Owain fares forth himself in quest of the fountain. Chrétien de Troyes, in his version of this adventure, the *Cheualier au Lyon*, places the fountain in the enchanted Forest of Broceliande. It was the Woodward of Broceliande Sir Kynon had encountered.

The Breton description of this Woodward of Broceliande is even more sinister than the Welsh:

"The lord of this vast forest was a terrible giant, completely black, who had only one foot and one eye. The animals, as well as the plants and the elements, obeyed him. At his will – at a word of command or a gesture of his hand – a thick mist filled glades; the trees appeared to be on fire; dreadful roarings arose on every hand, made even more appalling by their reverberating echoes; monsters issued from fathomless caves; hideous serpents entwined their folds about the blazing tree-trunks.

"Anyone who ventured to the heart of this immense, mysterious domain saw the trees begin to move and approach each other behind him, to close the way by which he had come and keep him forever a prisoner in this Valley of no Return."

The Briton legends give precise details as to the location and extent of this enchanted forest. It was nearly thirty leagues long and more than twenty leagues wide, and it covered the entire heart of the Amorican peninsula, its northern boundary stretching from Foug-ères to Quintin, its southern one from le Faouët to Redon. Arthur's camp (marked still by the *Grotte d'Arthus* at Huelgoat) was just outside its western extremity, his castle of Kerdhuel just beyond its north-ern boundary; Nantes, which Wolfram von Eschenbach gives as the chief seat of the Round Table in France, was a little further south-east of the forest's south-east corner. Thus a kind of Arthurian Gulf Stream engirdled and isolated it.

Today only scattered strips of Broceliande remain, the twelve thousand acres of Paimpont Forest, south of Rennes, being the largest. It is surely significant that Paimpont Forest is the scene of the Breton Grail-fairy-tale, *Peronnik l'Idiot*.

In terms of geological time, the separation of the British Isles from the continent of Europe took place compara-tively recently; formerly they and Brittany and the mid-western continental seaboard had been united in the ancient region of Hibernia. In Hibernia, when the

Manu led his chosen band from the sinking continent of Atlantis to the Tarim Basin near the Gobi Desert, last survivors of the Atlantean cataclysm found refuge.

The Hibernian Mysteries were of so lofty a spirituality that the Druids of the Celtic peoples, when these later came in their turn, united their wisdom with their own. But alongside these exalted Mysteries, relics of an atavistic Atlantean consciousness lingered wrongfully and harmfully into post-Atlantean times.

In the Woodward of Broceliande we can recognize many such atavistic echoes – in his single eye, the Atlantean clairvoyance; in his colour; its blotted-out dream-consciousness; in his size, the tendency innate in its strong lunar forces to produce gigantic forms, particularly in beings of evil disposition. The Atlanteans saw all things swathed in mist; to them the trees burned with an auric fire; so complete was their control of the Nature-forces that, as with the Woodward, animals plants and elements obeyed them.

Just as the Addnac slain by Peredur in the Welsh mabinogi which bears his name would seem to have been an anachronistic survival of the Avanc which in Welsh mythology had caused the Flood, so the monsters which at the Woodward's will issued from the fathomless caves of Broceliande and the hideous serpents entwining their folds about its blazing tree-trunks give the impression of being the terrible and illicit spawn of the decadent relics of an earlier phase of evolution.

The Atlanteans left behind were those who, through the betrayal of their Mysteries, had become the most depraved. Their dying-out filled all these ancient parts of the earth with devastating corruption which brought forth demonic beings; these it was the task of the Arthur

Mysteries to subdue. In Broceliande, with its one-eyed Woodward, we can see a kind of prototypal picture of a region still dominated by such evil astral forces, which the Arthurian knights exorcised in the shape of those nightmare monsters who issued from fathomless caves. The Arthurian cycles have come down to us clothed in pictures of medieval chivalry, so that we tend to forget the antiquity of the spiritual stream of which they bring us dim and distant rumours. "The content of the King Arthur legend, referred to in later times by scholarship which is not at all scholarly in respect of the real facts, reaches back in reality to a very early epoch," Rudolf Steiner tells us. He speaks of "a few thousand years ago, when the Arthur stream had its beginning," and of "the Arthur Impulse going out from England, an Impulse which was kindled originally by the Hibernian Mysteries."

Indeed, the reason given in the twelfth century for the institution of the Round Table points right back to the results of the ravishing of the nature-forces in the betrayed Atlantean Mysteries:

"In the wells and springs of England harboured damsels who fed the wayfarer with meat and bread. These maidens dwelt in caverns – which the old tale elsewhere calls grottoes – hewn out by more than mortal art in the depths of the forests...To Aaron there came out of the grotto a maiden – I trow you could not have wished for one more fair – and in her hand she bore a golden chalice. But Aaron* did wrong to her, and carried off her golden cup, and the men of Aaron* followed his evil example, so that springs dried up, and the grass withered, and never more came damsels out of the grottoes to comfort the wanderer." ... The Knights of the Round Table, "when they heard the tale, were at once

* Or Amangons

filled with a desire to win back the grottoes and restore
them to those hands which formerly had possessed
them."

For the relationship between nature-spirits and these
Mystery-messengers whom we call, in the term of a
later chivalry, Arthurian knights was a close and wonderful one. The knights received the working and weaving of the nature-beings into their own etheric bodies,
and with these nature-forces they received impulses
which came from the Sun, which in those pre-Christian
days they knew to be the dwelling-place of the Christ. It
was with the Christ Sun-forces thus borne to them by
the nature-beings that they were able to carry out their
task of battling with the astral beasts and uplifting and
civilising the peoples of Northern, Central and Western
Europe.

The Cernussos panel of the Gundestrup Bowl is like a
picture of this transformation.

This Celtic stag-god was an annunciation of the as yet
unincarnated Sun-being – we shall see presently how
the stag as image of the Sun-Christ echoed right down
the ages to *Perceval li Gallois* in the thirteenth century
and *Le Morte d'Arthur* in the fifteenth. In the panel he
sits cross-legged, his soles not yet belonging to the
Earth; in his left hand, the Luciferic hand, he grasps the
ram-headed serpent of the pre-Christian Luciferic wisdom which already searches forward towards the Lamb
of God. The torc of lordship in his right hand describes
the circle of the Sun.

He is the new Woodward of Broceliande. Under his
lordship hideous monsters no longer issue from fathomless caves, but the woodland creatures sport about him;
a nature-being rides gaily on a dolphin, that symbol of
transition, sacred to the sun; and a delicate uniting

tracery of leaves tells of a healed plant-world's rest-
oration of life-bestowing saps.

Once Rudolf Steiner has revealed to us this beautiful
and moving liaison between the nature-beings and the
Arthurian mission, we read with a new kindling of the
eye that

"In the old daïes of the King Arthoùre,
Of which that Bretons speken grete honoùre,
Al was this land fulfild of fayerie."

Or that:
"In these times there were fairies with knowledge of
enchantments and charms and acquainted with the powers of words and of stones and of herbs. These were
more numerous within the bounds of Great Britain than
in any other land."
We read now with a most willing suspension of disbelief
about Arthur's non-mortal godparents:

"As soon as he came to Earth,
Elves took him and enchanted him with magic
most strong.
They gave him to be the best of the knights.
They gave him to be a rich king.
They gave him to live long.
They gave him the princely virtues most good,
So that he was most generous of all men alive.
This the elves gave him;
And thus the child thrived."

We read with moved heart Arthur's last words:
"I will fare to Avalon, the fairest of all maidens, to

Argante the queen, an elf most fair; and she shall make my wounds all sound, make me whole with healing draughts. And afterwards I will come again to my kingdom, and dwell with the Britons with much joy."

We take seriously Layamon's declaration that Arthur's burny (coat of mail) was "fashioned of steel, that an elvish smith had made with his excellent craft; he was named Wygar, the witty wright (skillful craftsman)."

And we remember with a new understanding that it was the Lady of the Lake who brought up Sir Launcelot; that it was her arm clothed in white samite which, rising from the surface of the lake, both gave and received back Arthur's sword, Excalibur; and that it was she, under her Armorican name of Viviane, who, beside Sir Kynon's Fountain of Baranton in Cernussos' Forest of Broceliande, wove about Merlin that tower of invisible crystal in which the clear soul of the initiate unites with the transparency of the etheric world.

At the turning-point of time, Christ descended from the Sun. But the Round Table still continued to experience Him in Nature. "After the Mystery of Golgotha," Rudolf Steiner tells us, "the Earth was swathed by the Life-Sprit of the Christ. This was perceived in the Irish Mysteries, but above all by the Knights of King Arthur's Round Table, who lived within its Life-Spirit which encircled the Earth and in which there was this constant interplay of the Spirits of the Elements from about and from below... The Mystery of Golgotha legible in the Book of Nature represented the science of the higher graduates of King Arthur's Round table."

Thus the pre-Christian Christ-Stream of the Arthur

Mysteries was metamorphosed by the Mystery of Golgotha into a stream within Celtic Christianity; both were still cosmic.

With Christ had descended that cosmic intelligence which, administered by Michael, had hitherto inspired men in the sun-rays, but which had now to fall from his hands and become an earthly attribute. But the Round Table, itself a picture of the cosmos, an earthly reflection of the heavenly Zodiac, still clung to the cosmic intelligence, working longer than any other Michael-community to keep it still in Michael's hands.

The Norman tympanum at Parwich in Derbyshire, framed in its arch's chevron-portrayal of the light-ether, is like a soul-picture of the Arthur stream now Christ had come to earth. The Lamb of God has succeeded Cernussos as Woodward; the bird of thought hovers above Him; the stag, His forerunner, stands in homage before him, his antlers metamorphosed into great deep-ribbed leaves. The day-serpent and the night-serpent begin to intertwine man's sleeping and his waking into the healing caduceus of the second half of the Earth's evolution and to breathe forth *ur*-plant forms pointing to that Mercury dissolution which will release the archetypes frozen into matter by Mars in the earlier half. As, with the Persians, new life in the form of plants sprang from the back and tail of the bull when the sun-hero Mithras (their reflection of Michael) bestrode him, so here too the wild beast's tail breaks into leaf, into quicksilver-shaped leaf. But the cross the Lamb carries is still circled with the Celtic sun-torc, it is still the cross of the *Cosmic* Christ.

In the fourth century A.D. men carried the cosmic intelligence a first step in the direction of the modern intellect – the old clairvoyant picture-consciousness began to grow shadowy.

Till that century higher beings had been able to guide man through the more powerful upper portion of his astral body. But now the lower portion began to grow more powerful, increasing man's freedom but at the cost of sickness.

In the fourth century, also, the last of the old pre-Christian Mysteries declined, and at the same time the esoteric significance of the new Christian Mystery began to be largely lost. Julian the Apostate, the last human being who would have led the former Sun Mysteries over into the latter, was murdered in 363 A.D.

Further, from the beginning of that century, there began to fade that tableau of the life of Christ on Earth which till then had remained visible in the supersensible worlds and out of perception of which the Gospels had been written, men had a sense of being left lonely and bereft.

With the Arthurian knights this supersensible vision lasted longer; but after the first five centuries of our era, their powers also began gradually to diminish. "The King waxed slothful, and the Knights of the Round table, when they saw his well-doing slacken, departed thence and began to hold aloof from his Court, nor did no adventure befal there any more."

On Ascension Day the Queen begs him, weeping:

"Sir, were you to go to the chapel of S. Augustine that is in the White Forest, that may not be found save by adventure only, methinketh that on your back-repair you would again have your desire of well-doing."

King Arthur goes, and, kneeling at the door of the

chapel, sees a vision of the Child and His Mother as the hermit sings mass, and the hermit is the only living being in the chapel who is clothed in "deadly flesh." Yet the King hears "right fair responses, as it were the responses of angels... When the mass was sung, the voice of a holy angel said, *Ite, missa est.* The Son took the Mother by the hand, and they vanished forth of the chapel with the greatest company and the fairest that might ever be seen.'

And after this the King does indeed "amend him well;" and Sir Gawain and Sir Lancelot "have more toil and travail than all the knights in the world before them," and Sir Perceval "knoweth not how to live without travail, and little toil he thinketh of it, whereof shall God be well pleased.

We ask ourselves:

Why (as the Queen had prophesied) did the King's presence at mass at S. Augustine's chapel usher in a resuscitation of that knightly adventure which Rudolf Steiner characterises as "what the knights did in the fulfilment of their tasks"?

We learn from Rudolf Steiner's spiritual researches that from the fourth and fifth centuries onward, new elementary Spiritual Beings have been descending from other spheres to help men on earth. From that period when the lower portion of man's astral body began to pre-ponderate perilously in power, these new Earth-Spirits have so worked on men who had strong moral ideas as to build these moral ideas into their very being and blood, thus uniting a man's individual moral quality with his new and increasing individual freedom.

Such a process of creative fusion would seem to have come to birth in Arthur at the chapel of S. Augustine.

The chapel of S. Augustine "may not be found save by adventure only" – that is, in connection with the fulfilment of appointed tasks. What King Arthur experiences there implements his intention – "To amend me have I come hither." On his "back-repair" to court, not only his "*desire* of well-doing" but also his *power* of well-doing has been restored. It is exactly as if these new Earth-Spirits have become his helpers.

We ask ourselves again:

Why should this happen when the King is present at mass?

These new Earth-spirits find a path to man through ritual. Rudolf Steiner tells us that "in the cults of the Churches, those who have vision of realities can often dispense with the person who stands in the flesh before the altar, because – apart altogether from the officiating priests – they are able to perceive the presence of these Spiritual Beings in the ceremonies."

One is left with the awed surmise:

Can these new Earth-Spirits then have been "that greatest company and the fairest that might ever be seen" who made "right fair responses, as it were the responses of angels," and who had "evanished forth of the chapel" with the Son and His Mother when mass had been sung?

If one reads attentively one discovers how, from now on, delicate and gradual preparation is made for the far-off meeting and uniting of the Arthur stream with the Grail stream.

First, "when the hermit had done his service and was divested of the arms of God," he brings to King Arthur his first intimations of the Grail Quest:

"A great sorrow is befallen on the land of late through a young knight that was harboured in the hostel of the rich King Fisherman, for that the most Holy Graal appeared to him, yet never asked he to whom was served thereof from whence it came and for that he asked it not are all the lands commoved to war, nor no knight meeteth other in the forest but he runneth upon him and slayeth him."

Then, as Arthur rides home to Cardoil, " in the thick of the forest, he heard a Voice that began to cry aloud:

"King Arthur of Great Britain, God biddeth thee that thou hold court at the earliest thou mayest, for the world, that is now made worse of thee and of thy slackness in well-doing, shall thereof be greatly amended."

It had formerly been King Arthur's custom to hold court three times a year, at Christmastide, at Easter and at Pentecost; but after "a slothful will came upon him he had been no more minded to hold them." It was now Ascension-tide, ten days only till Pentecost: he therefore "made seal of his letters and sent them throughout all his lands that he would hold court at the feast of St. John, for that Whitsuntide was already too nigh. Wherefore all began now to marvel whence his new desire had come."

So, for the first and only time, Arthur held his court on S. John's Day, the day of him who said: "I (the last of the pre-Christian Sun-forces) must decrease, and He (the newly incarnated Sun) must increase." And it was on this day that the Grail Cross – the cross of the Christ Who had united Himself with the Earth – was first brought to Arthur's court.

For as Arthur and his knights sat at the table, three damsels entered the hall. The second damsel "bore at her neck a shield banded argent and azure with a red cross, and the boss was of gold, all set with precious stones." The first damsel said:

"Sir, the shield that this damsel beareth belonged to Joseph, the good soldier knight who took down Our Lord of hanging on the rood. Keep the shield for a knight that shall come hither for the same; you shall make it hang on this column in the midst of your hall, and guard it in such a wise as that none may take it save he only. And of this shield shall he achieve the Graal; and another shield shall he leave here in the hall, red, with a white hart."

The damsel brings King Arthur greetings from "the rich King Fisherman, of whom is sore sorrow for that he hath fallen into grievous languishment.

"'Damsel,' saith the King, 'sore pity it is; and God grant him his heart's desire.'

"'Sir,' saith she, 'know you wherefore he hath fallen into languishment?'

"'Nay, I know not at all, but gladly would I learn.'

"'This languishment is come upon him through one that harboured in his hostel, to whom the most Holy Graal appeared…'"

So King Arthur learns that King Fisherman's afflictions, like the wars and anarchy of which the hermit has told him, are due to the unasked Grail-question.

Much time was to pass and many adventures were to befall before, one night, King Arthur awoke and saw a ship "coming afar off as it were the shining of a candle in the midst of the sea. When the ship was arrived under the palace and was quite still, he saw therein a knight that lay all armed upon a table of ivory, and his hands were crossed upon his breast. Anon he cometh all armed and holding his sword all naked, and the King seeth that he beareth the red shield with the white hart whereof he had heard tell. The Knight taketh the shield that hung at the column and hangeth the other there; he enters again into the ship and so departs and leaves the castle behind.

"When Lancelot seeth the shield that he had left on the column, he knoweth it well, and saith: 'Now know I well that Perceval hath been here, for this shield was he wont to bear.'"

Thus Perceval, in this version of the lineage of "Joseph of Aberimacie", and in this version the first Arthurian knight in whose destiny Arthur-stream and the Grail-stream are to be united, is also the first for whom the white hart of the Cernussos who is the reflection of the Sun-Christ gives place to the Christ Who has become the Being of the Earth. This exchange takes place by night – that is, it is a supersensible experience; and at this point of time it takes place for him alone.

Galahad, in Malory the first Arthurian knight to achieve the Quest of the Grail, has a similar experience, one even more explicit. But in his case it is a mystical experience, and he shares it with the three human beings whose Grail destinies are most closely entwined with his own.

Galahad, with Bors, Percivale and Percivale's sister, was riding through a waste forest when "they saw afore them a white hart which four lions led." These they followed to a chapel, where a hermit sang mass.

"And at the secrets of the mass they saw the hart become a man and set him upon the altar in a rich siege; and saw the four lions were changed, the one to the form of a man, the other to the form of a lion, the third to an eagle, and fourth to an ox.

"Then took they their siege where the hart sat down and went out through a glass window, and there was nothing perished nor broken. And they heard a voice say: In such a manner entered the Son of God in the Womb of a maid Mary, whose virginity was ne perished ne hurt. And when they heard these words they fell down to the earth; and therewith was a great clereness."

When they "were come to theirself again," the hermit explained to them that by the four lions were to be understood the four Evangelists, and that "ofttimes or this Our Lord showed Him unto good men in likeness of an hart; but I suppose that from henceforth ye shall see Him no more."

Galahad, like Perceval, also had a red cross shield; like Perceval's Galahad's had also belonged to Joseph of Arimathea. Joseph had given it to the noble pagan, King Evelake, and had drawn the red cross upon it with his own blood. Galahad, like Perceval, is physically related to Joseph; but he is also descended from Evelake. The pagan piety of the one and the Grail guardianship of the other are already united in his blood.

In *Perceval li Gallois*, Perceval never asks the healing question of King Fisherman; but after the latter's death he rescues his castle and kingdom from the infidels who have conquered them under the King of Castle Mortal. Then "the Graal presented itself again in the castle, and the lance whereof the point bleedeth, and the other holy relics whereof was right great plenty. For our Lord God loved the place much."

At Whitsuntide King Arthur, holding his court at Cardoil, "looketh at the windows of the hall go right and left, and seeth that two sunbeams are shining within that fill the whole hall with light. Thereof he marvelleth much and sendeth without the hall to see what it might be. The messenger cometh back and saith thereof that two suns appear to be shining, the one in the East and the other in the West. He marvelleth much thereat.

"Then a Voice at one of the windows said to him: 'King, marvel not that two suns should appear in the sky. Know well that this is for joy of the conquest that the Good Knight hath made that took away the shield from herewithin. He hath won the land that belonged to good King Fisherman from the evil King of Castle Mortal, and therefore was it that the Graal was hidden. Now God so willeth that you go hither, and that you choose out the best knights of your court; for better pilgrimage may you never make; and what time you shall return hither, your faith shall be doubled and the people of Great Britain shall be better disposed and better taught to maintain the service of the Saviour.'"

When did two suns appear at the same time in the sky, the one in the East and other in the West? When did the Round Table go on pilgrimage to the Grail Castle? Rudolf Steiner tells us:

"Two streams came to meet each other – the pre-Christian Christ stream and the Christian Christ stream. The one is known subsequently as the Arthur stream, the other as the Grail stream. In the Christianity of the Grail, the Christ Who descended through the Mystery of Golgotha took His way from East to West. And to meet Him from the West there came the spiritual etheric image of the Christ evoked by the Mys-

tery of Golgotha but still picturing the Christ of the Sun
Mysteries.

"Form the West came pagan Christianity, the Arthur-
Christianity. From the East came the Christ in the
hearts of men.

"And then the meeting takes place.

"This meeting took place in the year 869 A.D."

When this momentous meeting took place, the cosmic
intelligence had taken a further earthward step. From
now on, for the next thousand years, western Christianity was to be formulated into exoteric dogma; there was
place in it neither for Arthurian understanding of the
Sun Mysteries nor for Grail understanding of Christ as
Spirit of the Earth. So these two streams flowed underground together, preserving their content in readiness
for the renewal of esoteric Christianity which would
accompany Michael's return to rulership of the Earth in
1879.

We live today in this new Michael age.

But before we can regain an understanding of Christ as
Sun-being and as Spirit of the Earth, that cosmic intelligence which had fallen from Michael's hands into
men's heads must return to him, that he may adminis-
ter it now through their hearts. And this, Rudolf Steiner
tells us, is to begin in our own time.

As, in the crisis in the fourth century, new Earth-spirits
descended from other worlds to help man build his
moral ideas into his blood, so, when the new Michael
Age began, further new Beings – Vulcan Beings –
began to descend to help man work on his now earth-
dried intellect and render it fit for Michael's service.

They bring us living Imaginations to quicken the corpses of our thinking into new life. They bring us cosmic truths ensouled in these Imaginations. They bring us Anthroposophy.

And more and more such beings will descend to help us in the coming centuries.

Twenty years after the beginning of the new Michael Age came the end of Kali Yuga. And with the end of Kali Yuga, the Dark Age, appeared a new kingdom of *Nature-Beings*, "in order that our life of soul may be quickened by what it draws from Nature."

The double thread of man's mortal life and the intellect's need of redemption runs through his connection with all three of these groups of new Beings on the earth. The new Earth-Spirits of the fourth and fifth centuries, who unite man's moral ideas with his growing freedom and who will help him to form the new earth-planet, Jupiter, out of his outbreathed morality, are "repelled by the brains of academic scholars and rebuffed by mechanical contrivances." The new Vulcan-Beings who from 1879 onwards seek to enliven the shadow-pictures of the intellect and to guide our thinking again into the sphere of Michael are also concerned that the Spiritual Science they bring to us "shall be translated onto social behaviour and action on the earth." And the new Kingdom of Elemental Beings who from 1899 issue from Nature as a fount of spiritual life bring changes into the ether-body both by the freshening forces with which they imbue our thinking and through the order brought to our moral impulses by the vision of the karma of our deeds which can be fostered in our souls when we carry these new helpers with us from Autumn through to Spring.

The ether-body is the instrument of our whole life of thought. The intellectuality of our own era has, up to this century, gradually dried and hardened this body as it has dried and hardened the physical one; but it has at the same time caused it to evolve towards a certain independence.

Once we have unfolded the faculty of thinking our own thoughts, our thinking is no longer limited to and by our sense impressions and the outer world. The world of thought can now embrace other worlds. And particularly if those worlds include the moral and the aesthetic, the ether-body slowly embarks on a process of loosening which can bring it eventually to actual perception in those other worlds.

The glorious crown of that long development will be, sometime in the future, the ability to perceive the Etheric Christ as a natural event.

When we consciously co-operate with our spiritual helpers, as the Arthurian knights did with theirs, we enter this true stream of future evolution. And as the Cernussos of the Gundestrup Bowl is like a picturing forth of the Christ of the Sun as He worked in these knights through those helpers; as the Norman tympanum at Parwich is like a picturing forth of the Cosmic Christ, now incarnated but still seen as the Sun-Spirit, bringing peace to the astral realm; so the Norman tympanum at Stoke-sub-Hamdon in Somerset is like a picturing forth of this true stream of future evolution.

In it the tree of Life has been restored to man and Nature. Because purified feeling leads to sense-free thinking, the earthly animals are no longer portrayed, but birds alight on the Tree. In the realm of the starry

animals, Sagittarius, that centaur-image of supersensible man, yearns towards Leo, the Sun-Portal through
which divine beings descend to earth. And the Christ
Himself appears in the etheric world, no longer as that
Sun-Being Image of Himself so long perceptible to
Arthurian vision, but as the Mystical Lamb, a Being so
cosmic that He sends us His sacrificial gifts from Aries,
but bearing now, in place of the Sun-Cross, that Cross
which He Bore when He rose from the grave as Spirit of
the Earth.

We see Him guarding with a lamb's gentle mien the
resurrected Tree of Life. We see in Him the world's true
Woodward.

REFERENCES

The Mabinogian (11th century), Lady Charlotte Guest's translation.
Légendes Tradionalles de la Bretagne, Louis Aubert.
Le Conte du Graal, Chrétien de Troyes (1188-1190).
Chaucer, (14th century).
Roman van Lanzelet, (12th century).
Brut, Layamon (1204).
Perceval li Gallois, (13th century), translated by Dr. Sebastian Evans as *The High History of the Holy Graal*.
Le Morte d'Arthur, Sir Thomas Malory (written 1467, printed 1485).

LECTURE-CYCLES by RUDOLF STEINER:

Karmic Relationships Vol. 8,
  Torquay, 12-21 Aug. 1924. (R. Steiner Press).

Karmic Relationships, Vol. 4,
  Dornach, 5-23 Sept. 1924.

Supersensible Influences in the History of Mankind,
  Dornach, 22nd Sept. – 1st Oct. 1922. (R. Steiner Press).

A Picture of Earth Evolution in the Future,
  see in "Materialism and the Task of Anthroposophy",
  Dornach, 13th May 1921, (Anthroposophic Press) .

The Christ Impulse in the Course of History,
  see "Esoteric Christianity",
  Lugano 17 Sept. 1911 and Locarno 19 Sept. 1911.
  (R. Steiner Press).

FOOTNOTE REGARDING REFERENCES:

In the references to this first chapter as in all subsequent chapters, dates have been given to help readers identify references to Rudolf Steiner's works.

With regard to the various manuscripts containing the legends, publishers and dates of publication are not given, as there are a number of versions currently available.

Isabel Wyatt

ADDITIONAL FOOTNOTE
to the 2005 edition:

A complete list of references for the whole book, in alphabetical order, is given at the end of the book (pages 264-266).

There follows a numerical guide of references for each individual chapter, in the order in which they have been used by the author (page 267). This may both aid the reader's understanding of the text and also perhaps encourage further studies.

Siegfried Rudel

CHAPTER II

THE MARVELLOUS CUSTOM OF KING ARTHUR'S SON

An aura of reticence and mystery surrounds King Arthur's son. Arthurian literature tells us much concerning other leading knights – Gawain, Perceval, Kay, Tristan, Bors, Bedivere, Galahad; in striking contrast, it tells us singularly little concerning Lohot. Yet that little clearly indicates that he belongs to the Round Table's innermost, most esoteric circle.

Thus, the Welsh Triads laud him, under the Welsh form of his name, as one of the "Three Learned Ones of the island of Britain – Gwalchmai ab Gwyar (Gawain), Llacheu ab Arthur (Lohot), and Rhiwallon with the broom-blossom hair; there was nothing of which these three did not know the elements and the material essence."

He is not only learned; he is also wise in counsel. When, in a Welsh mabinogi, Olsa Gyllellvawr craves a truce of Arthur, Llacheu the son of Arthur is among the King's advisers assembled to consider the petition.

When Chrétien de Troyes sets out to "tell you the names of some of the best of the knights who belonged to the Round Table", he includes "a young man of great merit, Loholt the son of King Arthur,"

And in the thirteenth century French romance, *Perceval*

li Gallois, when Perceval, himself to be the Best Knight in the world, hears of Lohot's death, he mourns the passing of one excelling in knightly prowess – "This is sore pity of the King's son, that he is dead in such manner, for ever he waxed more and more in great chivalry."

In this romance we never meet Lohot in the flesh; we only hear of him. Yet what we hear of him is intimately bound up with Perceval's destiny and with the preparation for the meeting of the Arthur stream with the Grail stream, and would even seem delicately to point forward to present and future phases in human evolution. We first hear of Lohot when, on Gwain's and Lancelot's return to the Court at Cardoil, King Arthur asks them whether they have met "Lohot, my son, in none of these islands nor in none of these forests", and they assure him they have met him nowhere. He then tells them that Lohot had ridden forth to find and fight the giant Logrin, "who did my land more hurt than any other." But Kay the Seneschal has just returned to Court, bearing at his saddle-bow the head of Logrin, with the announcement that he himself had slain the giant, "whereof I made great joy, but marvel much what hath become of Lohot, for no tidings have I heard of him since he rode forth.

Meanwhile, Perceval has come by ship to the castle at dead of night, to exchange his Arthurian shield "of sinople, with a white hart," for the Grail shield, "banded azure and argent, with a red cross thereon and a boss of gold," which a damsel had left hanging on a column for him. From this moment onward, Perceval's adventures take on more and more Grail significance; and as the story unfolds we are made aware that with no shield except the Grail shield could Lohot's unfinished task be carried forward to completion.

Riding alone through strange forests, Perceval comes to a land laid waste and "void of folk." Its only sign of life is a little hermitage built in a mountain combe.

Dismounting at its chapel's open door, he sees a pall spread before the altar and hears the hermit singing the Mass for the Dead.

Perceval kneels in the doorway till the mass is ended and the hermit come to greet him. Then he learns that the mass at which he has been present was sung for Lohot, King Arthur's son, who lies buried beneath the pall; that it was the giant Logrin who had laid waste the surrounding countryside; and that Lohot had tracked the giant hither and slain him in fair fight.

"But Lohot had a marvellous custom," the hermit continued. "When he had slain a man, he slept upon him. Kay the Seneschal was come into the forest; he heard the giant roar when Lohot struck him the mortal blow. Thither came he as fast as he might, and found the King's son sleeping upon Logrin.

"He drew his sword, and therewith cut off Lohot's head, and set the head and body in a coffin of stone, then cut off the giant's head, that was right huge and hideous, and hung it at his saddle-bow, and so departed."

A damsel had come and taken away Lohot's head in a little coffer smelling sweetly of balsams and set with precious stones. But first she had helped the hermit to remove Lohot's body from the coffin of stone and bear it into the chapel and enshroud and bury it before the altar.

How are we to understand Lohot's marvellous custom?

When he had slain a man, he slept upon him. We are surely here concerned with the mysteries of sleep and death.

In sleep a man's inner being goes forth temporarily from his outer sheath; In death a man's inner being slowly withdraws from that outer sheath for ever. All men enter the starry realms in sleep; but only those who are on a path of spiritual development do so consciously.

As one on such a path, Lohot enters the world of sleep which is also the world of the dead not in the customary state of unconsciousness of today, but in a full awareness in which he is able to behold the realm of the supersensible and to feel united with the beings and the deeds of those he meets there, when he sleeps on the body of a man whom he has slain, the two inner beings of slayer and slain emerge from their outer sheaths together, to meet and mingle in a realm where other values rule than those of earth.

Meeting on such a plane, both see how Karma plays into the slaying – not only the possible karma working out of the past, but also the certain karma laid up by the deed for the future. So Lohot may be thought of as already possessing in sleep that faculty which Rudolf Steiner tells us has to be developed in our time in waking consciousness – the perception in picture-form of the karmic counterpart of a deed we have just done.

Lohot thus gains interest in the other, and the other in him. Steiner characterises a heightened interest in each other as the foundation-stone of the new morality we must also begin to develop in our time – "not subjectively, in man's usual indolent fashion, but suddenly, as with a leap, through the spiritual infusion of a certain secret: what the other man is. I mean by this something

concrete, not a theoretical abstraction."
In Lohot's slaying-sleep, then, two egos now (if not
before) karmically connected meet naked and face to
face, their clear vision of each other no longer clouded
by their physical eyes.

Lohot, then, is here shown as experiencing the mysteries of sleep and death. Astonishingly – yet why
should we be astonished? – it is in connection with just
these mysteries that we meet with him again in the
English folk-tale, Jack the Giant-killer.
"Now it happened in these days that King Arthur's
only son was journeying into Wales, in search of a
beautiful lady who was possessed with seven evil spirits.
His father had given him two horses, one for him to
ride, the other laden with money. He came to a
market-town, where he beheld a vast crowd of people
arresting the corpse of a man who died owing large
sums of money."
King Arthur's son bade them bury the corpse and come
to himself for payment of their debts. They came in
such numbers that by nightfall he had only two pence
left.
"Now Jack the Giant-killer, coming that way, was so
taken with the generosity of the Prince that he desired
to be his servant; and next morning they set forward on
their journey together. As they rode out of town, an
old woman called out that the dead man had owed her
two pence these seven years. So the Prince gave her all
he had left."
King Arthur's son spends all his treasure in ransoming
the debts of a dead man – that is, in taking his unpaid

Karma on himself. And that very deed attracts and devotes to his service the very forces needed for his mission – the deliverance of the lady from the seven evil spirits who possess her.

For in seeking to serve King Arthur's son, Jack acquires four talismans. The first, the coat of darkness, renders him invisible – that is, he can remain conscious in the world of sleep. (King Arthur had a tartan which rendered him invisible; it was one of the Thirteen Treasures of Britain taken by Merlin into his house of glass on Bardsey Island and never seen again).

The second, the cap which tells him all he wishes to know; is the magical "thinking cap" of brain free cognition.

The third, a sword which cuts asunder whatever it strikes, is that spinal consciousness which works rightly during sleep but becomes a Cain weapon if wielded when awake. (In the Breton Grail-fairytale, *Peronnik l'Idiot*, Rogear the Magician keeps it by day in an underground vault in the form of a diamond lance and takes it out only by night.)

The shoes of extraordinary swiftness are a picture of mobility in supersensible spheres.

When King Arthur's son reaches the house of the beautiful lady possessed of the seven evil spirits, she sets him two tasks. The first evening she shows him her handkerchief and tells him that unless he can show it to her next morning he must lose his head.

"Jack's cap of knowledge told him how to obtain the handkerchief. In the middle of the night the lady called on her familiar spirit to carry her to Lucifer. But Jack put on his coat of darkness and his shoes of swiftness, and was there as soon as she was."

She gives the handkerchief to Lucifer, who lays it on a

shelf. Jack takes it unseen and brings it to King Arthur's son.

The second task is to show the lady the following morning the lips she will have kissed during the night. Again she goes to Lucifer's palace at midnight. There she kisses his lips. Jack has again followed her; when she has departed, he unsheathes the magic sword and cuts off Lucifer's head.

When, next morning, King Arthur's son shows Lucifer's head to the lady, "the seven evil spirits left her, and she appeared in all her beauty." King Arthur's son marries her; and she and Jack accompany him on his return to his father's Court.

We have seen that the task of the Knights of the Round Table was the civilising of Europe by the cleansing of the astral body of earlier post-Atlantean times through the exorcising of the demonic beings who dominated it. The beautiful lady of the folk tale is an occultly exact picture of human astrality not yet cleansed and brought into order. "Backward Luciferic beings of seven different kinds," Dr. Steiner tells us, "remained behind upon the Moon and worked upon the astral human body. We know that if our evolution is not carried out aright, it is owing to the power of these seven different kinds of Luciferic beings."

That the lady's evolution has not hitherto been carried out aright is indicated by her conscious association with Lucifer by night. It is true that between going to sleep and waking, men spend their lives in his company; but for all except those on a path of spiritual development a veil has hitherto been drawn over this experience. What

Jack experienced legitimately, the lady experienced illicitly.

But in 1899, when Kali Yuga ended, a new Age of Light began. The natural clairvoyance with which, from our time onwards, more and more men will be endowed, increasingly making visible to them the karmic counterpart of a deed they have just done and reaching its flowering in the perception of the Etheric Christ, will also dissolve the veil which in sleep now covers men with darkness.

Then Lucifer will be known to be our companion in sleep, as Ahriman is known to be when waking. Till now there had been a gulf fixed between these two lives, our life of sleeping and our life of waking, so that we have not been fully able to carry the gifts of either companion over into the domain of the other.

"Had we been able to carry our day-thoughts over into the night," Rudolf Steiner tells us, "we should now have had a living science." But now the possibility of this will begin to come to pass.

What will it be like, this living science? It will surely penetrate into the etheric world that underlies and sustains the world of physical phenomena. It will bring to birth in a new form suited to a new epoch that Lohot-knowledge of the Three Learned Ones of Britain – there will be nothing of which it will not know the elements and the material essence.

Lohot had slain the giant Logrin, and, betrayed by his marvellous custom, had himself been slain by Kay. But Logrin's destructive forces still worked on. For forth from Logrin's castle there presently issued one of his retinue quite literally breathing fire and slaughter, for his shield bore a living dragon's head which belched forth flame.

Tidings were brought to King Arthur that this Knight of the Fiery Dragon was ravaging the land in revenge for Logrin's death "He warreth upon you for love of him whose head Messire Kay brought you; nor never, saith he, will he have joy until he shall have avenged him on your body."

Just as, in the folk-tale, Lohot took over the dead man's debts, so Perceval, the only knight who had heard the Mass for the Dead sung for Lohot, now takes over Lohot's unfinished task.

It is a task which Lohot could bring only to a certain stage of completion, for he belongs to that Arthur stream which has not yet met the Grail stream and for which Christ remains still the Sun-Christ, whereas, as it now demonstrated with terrific impact, the only thing that can prevail against the Fiery Dragon is the blood Christ shed on the Earth.

The combat is described in a passage of immense power:

"The Knight of the Dragon cometh at Perceval with his drawn sword, which is a burning brand. Perceval goeth against him , spear in rest; the flame that issued from the Dragon's head on the Knight's shield burnt the staff thereof even to his hand.

"The Knight smiteth him on the top of his helmet, but Perceval covereth him of his shield. Great marvel hath the Knight that he had not dealt him his death-blow. He turneth the head of the Dragon towards Perceval's shield, but its flame turned back again as it had been blown of the wind.

"Perceval dealeth a blow on the Knight's shield that

cleaveth the Dragon's head, and the flame leapeth forth on his sword so that it waxed red-hot.

"Perceval smiteth the Dragon's head with his sword which is now all a flame of fire; and the Dragon's head hurleth forth a cry so huge that forest and fell resound thereof as far as two leagues Welsh, then turneth towards his Lord in great wrath and scorcheth him to dust, and thereafter departeth up into the sky like lightning."

It is by the might of his Grail-shield that Perceval escaped death from a thrust which has always before proved mortal. It is by the might of the shield that the Dragon's flame is turned back again as it had been blown of the wind. The secret of its sovereignty is revealed when we are told that: "Joseph of Abarimacie had made be sealed in the boss of the shield some of the blood of our Lord and a piece of His garment." The blood of Christ works microcosmically within the boss as it works macrocosmically within the earth itself.

It had been prophesied that only the Best Knight in the world could ever destroy the Fiery Dragon. Perceval had gone to this dread combat incognito, under the sobriquet of "The King of the Golden Circlet." When the tidings were brought forth to King Arthur that an unkown knight had slain his enemy, his heart cried out that this victor must be his son; not only therefore was Lohot still alive, but he was also the prophecy's Best Knight in the world. And so he was filled with double joy.

Meanwhile, Perceval's uncle, King Fisherman, has died, and the latter's evil brother, the King of Castle Mortal, has conquered the Graal Castle. The task now laid on Perceval by destiny is to win this castle back. Till he has done so, Grail stream and Arthur stream cannot meet and mingle.

Perceval's third uncle, King Hermit, gives him a banner and a white mule "starred on the forehead with a red cross," and tells him that he has nine bridges to take, each held by three knights, but that a white lion will help from the third bridge onwards. So, with only twelve hermits as companions in this adventure, Perceval sets out to recapture the Graal Castle.

As soon as he comes within sight, and the knights holding the first bridge perceive the red cross on his shield, they begin to tremble, "for long since had it been prophesied that he who bore such a shield should win the Graal." When he pauses beside Joseph of Arimathea's tomb, which stands on the way to the bridges, it opens and gives forth sweet savours; and at this miracle trepidation spreads from bridge to bridge.

So, riding the white mule, bearing the banner, accompanied by the white lion and followed by the twelve hermits, Perceval takes bridge after bridge, so sorely dismayed are their defenders "for dread of a single knight."

When the King of Castle Mortal saw that the Graal Castle was lost, he stood on its walls and smote himself with his sword, and his dead body plunged into the river, which ran swift and deep below. As Perceval and the hermits entered the master hall, they heard, from the empty chapel beyond, a chanting of *Gloria in excelsis Deo*. "And when the conquest of the castle was over, the Graal presented itself again in the chapel."

And now the threads are gathered together in a swift and deeply moving sequence of events.

As soon as Perceval has won back the Graal Castle, two suns appear in the sky to King Arthur and his Court, and a voice bids the King to go on pilgrimage to the Graal.

"And straightway, behold you, a damsel cometh,and she beareth a coffer richer than ever you saw." She tells King Arthur that it contains the head of a knight, and that only he who slew the knight can open the coffer. She begs that all the knights present should try, and that he who succeeds "shall have the grace of forty days after you return from the Graal."

The King tries first. He fails. All the knights sitting at the table with him try. All fail.

Kay the Seneschal had served at meat. He hears of the coffer, "and he comes hither, all uncalled for.

"'Ah, Kay,' saith the King, 'I had forgotten you.'

"You ought not to forget me.' saith Kay. 'I am as well able to open a coffer as these others.'

"'Kay,' saith the King,'will you be as merry if you do? I am fain it should not open for *me*.'

"'I would,' saith Kay, 'that all the heads of all the knights I have slain, save one only, were in the midst of this hall, and that there were letters sealed with them to say they were slain by me.'"

As soon as Kay touched the coffer, it opened, and a sweet smell came forth from it and filled the hall. Within could be seen a head, and beside it letters of gold.

"'Sir,' saith Kay to the King, 'now you may know of some prowess I have done in your service.'"

King Arthur bade his chaplain to read the letter aloud. He himself sat down beside the Queen, and all his knights with him; and all the hall was silent.

The chaplain scanned the letters. Then he sighs. Then he read aloud that this head was the head of Lohot, the King's son, and that he has been slain by Messire Kay the Seneschal.

When Queen Guenievre heard this, she swooned over the coffer. Then she took the head and gazed at it, holding it in her two hands, "and knew well that it was her son by the scar on his face. The King maketh dole that none may comfort him. Never did no man see greater dole made than they of the Round Table made for the youth."

Kay the Seneschal fled to Brittany, to King Arthur's enemy Briant of the Isles. Later they made war on Arthur together. All that followed of anarchy and heartbreak which in Malory stems from Mordred's treachery, in this version stems from Kay's beheading of Lohot.

Yet it was this beheading that made plain the way for the uniting of the Arthur stream and the Grail stream.

A beheading cuts off the past, for the head of one incarnation is built out of the will-forces of the previous one. But the beheading of his son was for King Arthur a cutting-off of the part of his future that was rooted in the past. The inherited forces of the Arthur stream had come to an end.

"When the mourning for the King's son was abated," Lancelot reminds King Arthur of "the pilgrimage to the most holy Graal God willeth you should go." The King replies that he will go right willingly, and begins to prepare for the pilgrimage. It is his wish that the Queen should go with you, "but for the mourning she made for her son none might give her any comfort."

Before Arthur departs on his pilgrimage, he has the head of Lohot taken to the Isle of Avalon and placed in the Chapel of Our Lady on the top of "the mountain" there.

Later, after the Queen's death, Lancelot comes to this chapel, and in it sees two rich coffins standing side by side, "and at the four corners four tall candles burning, with clerks chanting psalms in turn on the one side and the other."

One of the hermits tells Lancelot that the coffins were made for King Arthur and Queen Guenievre. In one lies her body; in the other lies the head of her son. It was her will that at King Arthur's death his body should also lie beside her own.

Later again, when the Graal pilgrimage had been made, King Arthur and Gawain, on their homeward journey, came to Avalon and lodge the night with the hermits there. "When the King seeth the coffin where the Queen lieth and that wherein lieth the head of his son, thereof is his dole renewed, and he saith that this holy place ought he of right to love better than all other places on earth."

What does it mean, that Lohot's head is preserved at Avalon?

Avalon, with its strange "mountain" rising within the circle of its giant earth-mound Zodiac, has a sanctity which reaches back into the dim mist of antiquity. Poems written by the historical prototype of Merlin point to its having been an ancient Mystery Centre. In such holy places were laid up the seeds of a new impulse, to be preserved till the time is ripe for them to germinate and flourish.

It is Kay who has beheaded Lohot. Steiner speaks of Kay as connected with the etheric body. We can perhaps see a hint of this in his office of Seneschal, for the etheric body is concerned, among other things, with nourishment.

It is also concerned with growth; and among the four elements its cosmic parallel is water. In these connections we can perhaps understand the magical feats which are attributed to Kay —that he could breathe nine days and nights under water, and that he could make himself as tall as the tallest tree in the forest. This latter feat also perhaps throws light on why Peredur, in the Welsh mabinogi which bears his name, invariably addresses Kay as "tall man", and why, in the Welsh Arthurian tales, Kay is known as "Kei the Long".

It is indeed the etheric body, in its own drying up and hardening over the past centuries, that has confined the Lohot-forces in a coffin of stone. But the damsel brought to King Arthur the head in which the organ of a future consciousness had been elaborated through Lohot's marvellous custom; and King Arthur laid it up in Avalon.

"Guenievre" in Welsh signified "White lady". To this Queen belongs the rhythm of the creative forces of that White Lady, the Moon, while its own forces, working against gravity from within the earth which they have penetrated, help man to elevate his inner being into the starry realms.

So, when Queens Guenievre has Lohot's head preserved in the coffin which she has prepared for King Arthur and which stands beside her own in the chapel on the

Tor at Avalon – King Arthur who is to be taken to this holy place to be healed of his wounds and from it is to come again when world-destiny demands his return – the delicate implication is there that in their due time the Lohot-forces also will awake out of their germinal sleep to fertilise future generations.

We have seen how Lohot's marvellous custom speaks with particular urgency to the changing conditions of our own times, with its archetypal seeds of new faculties due now to be sown in ourselves – that vision of the karmic counterpart of deeds just done which will bring order into our new morality; that deep soul-experience of each other which is to be this new morality's foundation; that carrying of our day-thoughts over into the night out of which will grow a new living science.

But those mysteries of sleep and death to which Lohot's marvellous custom was his portal also reverberate on into far, far vistas of evolution.

For in the Earth's next incarnation, Jupiter, this planet will consist wholly of man's outbreathed morality. All that is mineral, all that is material, will have fallen away. This means that our mineral, material physical bodies will also have fallen away.

The sword which cuts asunder whatever it strikes will exist no more; for the organic activity which it is now its rightful task to regulate in sleep will also exist no more. Sleep itself will exist no more. Our sense-organs, our brain-based thinking, our muscular mobility, will exist no more. They will be replaced by the coat of darkness, the shoes of swiftness, and the cap which tells us all we wish to know.

That state of disembodied awareness which now man enters only at death or in initiate sleep will on Jupiter be permanently his, heightened to a superconsciousness. Each time Lohot slept on one whom he had slain, he went out into this sphere of after-death, into a foreshadowing of this future Jupiter condition. In his marvellous custom we can see, a kind of Jupiter rehearsal, a sowing not only of seeds of our own era but also of the seed of Jupiter-man.

REFERENCES

The Dream of Rhonabwy.
Erec et Enide.
Jack the Giant-killer (The version quoted is from a
   Chap-book of 1805 in the British Museum).

LECTURES by RUDOLF STEINER:

The Work of the Angel in Man's Astral Body,
   Zurich, 9th Oct. 1918,
   also in "Angels" (R. Steiner Press).

Background to the Gospel of St. Mark,
   Berlin 17 Oct. 1910, 10 June 1911, Munich 23
   Dec. 1910, Hanover 18 Dec. 1910, Coblenz 2 Feb. 1911.
   (R. Steiner Press).

The Tree of Life and the Tree of Knowledge
   Dornach, 24 July-8 Aug. 1915, 24,25 July in
   "Golden Blade" 1965. The rest in typescript R 43.

CHAPTER III

THE ARTHURIAN PILGRIMAGE TO THE GRAAL

When,in *Perceval li Gallois*, two suns appear in the sky at King Arthur's Court, one in the East, the other in the West, and a Voice announces that Perceval has won the Graal Castle and that God wills Arthur to go on a pilgrimage thither with the best knights of his Court, Arthur chooses Lancelot and Gawain to accompany him,"with more knights, and taketh one squire to wait upon his body."

Arthur would have wished also to have had Queen Guenievre's company. But she is distraught with sorrow over the death of Lohot, her son. So he leaves her at the Court as Regent in his absence.

It is a small cavalcade of four which sets out on this momentous journey.

In individual human lives one can sometimes observe fulfilments of karma unfolding so thick and fast that one receives the strong impression that the working-out of personal karma is being accelerated in order that the hands may be free to be placed at the service of world-karma. A somewhat similar impression is received as one observes the adventures of this pilgrimage unfolding.

One adventure after another presents itself as the karma of an earlier event in Arthur's or Gawain's or Lancelot's life. It is as if our own newly dawning faculty of seeing in picture-form the karmic counterpart of a deed just done as being, in protoype, placed into outer life and exercise in concrete reality, and as if purely "Arthurian" karma were being met and paid in order that the new stage now approaching, may be embarked upon with freer hands. For the Arthurian visit to the Graal Castle is itself connected with world-karma; the meeting of the Arthur stream and the Grail stream is destined to work in a concealed but powerful fashion in the spiritual background of world-history to come.

Having ridden far the first day, the four pilgrims found themselves benighted in a forest "where was neither hold nor hermitage" in which they could seek harbourage for the night. The squire climbed a tall tree, and saw the glow of a fire a long way off. Towards this they rode, and, passing over a bridge of wattles, came into a deserted hall and sat down before the fire.

The squire, entering a side-chamber in search of bait for the horses, cries out in horror that it was heaped with dead men. Lancelot went in and found it was so.

A damsel entered from the forest, "her kirtle all torn with briars, her feet all bleeding for that she was unshod. She had a face of exceeding great beauty. She carried the half of a dead man, and cast it into the chamber with the others."

When she saw Lancelot, she cried joyfully:

"Ha, God, now am I quit of my penance! Sir, I am the damsel of the Castle of Beards, that was wont to deal with knights so foully. You did away with that toll, and had me in covenant that, so the Holy Graal should appear to you, you would come back. You returned not, for that you saw not the Graal. For the shame that I did to knights was this foul penance laid upon me until such time as you should come."

A rout of fiends in the shape of knights came rushing through the forest "as they would rend it all up by the riots". As they burst into the hall, Lancelot drew a circle round the house-place with his sword and within this they all five stood.

The fiends snatched up great blazing firebrands and hurled them within the circle, but the pilgrims held their shields against them and "smote the firebrands so that they made the red-hot charcoal fly". When they cut the fiend-knights "limb from limb, they turned to ashes, and devils all black came forth from their bodies".

A second rout of demon knights burst in, worse even than the first. "They began to press the King and his knights hard. While they were thus in the thickest of the conflict, they heard a bell sounding, and forthwith the fiends departed at a great pace".

The damsel told the King:

"Sir, this sound have I heard every night, whereby my life hath been saved."

In the morning the damsel took leave of them, and three hermits came to bury the dead men, "that the evil haunting might be stayed, and to build up the place in holiness for the service of God. The King was right joyful thereof".

We have spoken of the Arthurian mission of fighting and conquering demonic powers. In a poem written at Tintagel, where Arthur and his knights received the Sun-powers which enabled them to carry out this task, Rudolf Steiner characterises them as "warriors against demons". The writer of *Perceval li Gallois* therefore speaks with exactitude in his description of the fight in the charnel-house. Even that the demons encountered there are connected with the corpses of dead knights is in keeping with what Steiner tells us of the demons arising out of the corruption left when the depraved Atlantean bodies died out.

When we turn back the pages of Lancelot's life till we come to the incident of which this evil haunting was the karmic counterpart, we find it bound up with the astrality of the Damsel of Beards' evil custom; but we also find it bound up with a still unrepented and therefore still unredeemed astrality in Lancelot himself.

Lancelot had once come to a castle whose great gate was "all covered with beards fastened thereon, and heads of knights in great plenty hung thereby". Two knights issued from the gate and demanded Lancelot's beard, for such toll was custom of the castle. ("Sir, now pay us yours, for a great beard it is.") Lancelot, fighting to retain his beard, had sorely wounded them both; and the Lady of the Castle had come forth and bidden him enter. At table they had been served by knights maimed in hand or foot or eye.

The Lady of the Castle had tried her hardest to keep Lancelot with her; but he has told her:

"Lady, in no castle may I abide more than one night until I have been thither whither it behoveth me to go." For he was on his way to the Graal Castle, hoping to behold the Graal and, by asking whom it served, to heal King Fisherman of his languishment. But under pressure from the lady he had pledged his faith to return to her, should his Graal quest be achieved.

After further adventures, Lancelot had come to a hermitage at the foot of the mountain beyond which lay the Graal Castle. There he had alighted and made his confession. "He rehearseth all his sins, and saith that of all he repenteth, save only one, the fairest sin and the sweeteth that ever he committed."

"I love my lady, which is the Queen, more than aught else that liveth. The affection seemeth me so good and so high that I cannot let go thereof. I am willing to do penance as great as is enjoined of this sin, but my lady the Queen I will serve so long as it is her pleasure."

The hermit had warned him:

"So much am I fain to tell you, that if you shall lie in the hostel of King Fisherman, yet never may you behold the Graal for the mortal sin that lieth at your heart."

And even thus it had come to pass.

At the Graal Castle, King Fisherman, lying "on a bed so rich and so fair apparelled as never was seen a better," had conversed with Lancelot "right nobly, as one that is a right worshipful man. But when the table was dight of rich sets of vessels of gold and silver, and they were served of rich meats of venison of hart and wild boar, the Graal appeared not at this feast. Lancelot was one of the three knights of the world of the most renown and mightiest valour, but it held aloof for his great sin as touching the Queen, whom he loved without repenting him thereof."

When, later, Lancelot has come to the hermitage of King Fisherman's brother, King Hermit, the latter had told him plainly:

"Had you had the like desire to see the Graal that you have to see the Queen, the Graal would you have seen."

So, in the last resort, it was because of Lancelot's love of the Queen that the Lady of the Castle of Beards had been forced to do so long and foul a penance, and that he, with King Arthur, Gawain and the squire, had been forced to battle with the demon knights to clear the hall in the forest of its evil.

The four now "rode right busily on their journeys, and came to a little castle in a combe, and the enclosure of the castle was fallen down into an abysum". A priest tells that this is Tintagel, and King Arthur now hears the story of his own birth for the first time. "King Uther Pendragon slew King Gorlois on the morrow of the night he lay with his wife, and so forthwith espoused Queen Ygerne, and in such a manner was King Arthur conceived in sin that is now the best King in the World."

So Arthur gazes back upon his own beginnings as in a kind of life-panorama such as accompanies the death of the physical body and the birth of the soul into the spiritual world, or such as accompanies the mystical death and rebirth of initiation. Can we perhaps see in it such a life-panorama reviewed in preparation for the new birth of the Arthurian Mysteries into union with the Mysteries of the Grail?

And now the day draws near when Lancelot must
return to the Waste City to acquit him of a pledge.
He had come to the city on leaving the Castle of
Beards, and had found it "void of folk, great palaces
fallen down, and the gates ruined with age." A young
knight of great comeliness had approached him,
"clad in a short red jerkin with a rich girdle of gold; on
his head had he a great cap of gold, and he held a great
axe."
He said to Lancelot:
"Sir, needs must you cut off my head with this axe,
for of this weapon hath my death been adjudged."
Lancelot had reasoned with him; but the young knight
had insisted, imposing a condition in return:
Fair sir, hold up your hand towards the minster you see
yonder, and swear to me upon the holy relics that are
therein that on this day, at the house that you shall
have slain me, you will return and place your head in
the same peril."
Lancelot had so sworn, and the young knight had knelt
and had received the death-blow he had demanded.
Lancelot, coming to his horse, had looked behind him as
he mounted. Both the body and the head of the young
knight had disappeared.

And now "the King embraceth Lancelot at parting, and
Messire Gawain also, and they pray God preserve his
life, and that they may see him again ere long."
Lancelot rides again to the Waste City, and finds it as

empty as before. As he dismounts, a knight approaches, wearing a close-fitting jerkin and carrying the great axe. He bids Lancelot "come forward without delay and kneel down and stretch your neck, even as my brother did."

"Lancelot lieth down on the ground as it were on a cross, and crieth mercy to God. He taketh three blades of grass and eateth thereof in token of the holy communion, then signeth himself of the cross and blesseth him, riseth up, setteth himself on his knees and stretcheth forth his neck."

The first blow missed. As the knight is aiming a second, a cry rings out:

"Throw down the axe and cry the knight quit!"

Two damsels "of passing great beauty" come forward, saying to Lancelot:

"Sir, we are the two sisters that you saw so poor when you lay in our brother's house. You and Messire Gawain gave us the treasure and the hold of the robber-knights you slew. This city of our brother would never again be peopled of folk save a knight had come hither as loyal as are you. Had you failed us of your covenant, we should have lost this city and its castles without recovery."

These were the two sisters "of passing great beauty, right poorly clad," who, some months previously, had been in the act of welcoming Gawain to their brother's ruined castle, when a wounded knight brought tidings that Lancelot was sore beset nearby by four robber-knights. Gawain had departed "as fast as horse may carry him," and following the blood-track of the

wounded knight, had reached Lancelot in time to turn
the tide of battle.

When Gawain told Lancelot that he had "the most
poverty-stricken host he had ever seen," they agreed to
make him a gift of the robber-knights' ill-gotten gains –
"rich treasure, rich ornaments, rich armour for horses,
rich sets of vessels that they had thrown the one over
the other into a pit that was right broad."

Their rejoicing host had confessed, when they disarmed,
that he had no robe to lend them, "for none have I save
my own poor jerkin." The two damsels had taken off
their own kirtles, and "the two knights did on the kirtles, all to-torn and ragged and worn as they were."

So now separate threads out of the past are twined
together in the Waste City, which is no longer waste, for
the mystical decapitation of the young knight, and Lancelot's willingness to suffer the same sacrifice, bring
about a resuscitation of the city's dried-up life forces.

Lancelot, leaning at the windows of the hall, now "seeth
the city peopled of the fairest folk in the world, and
heareth how the greatest joy in the world is being made
in the forest, and the clerks and priests are coming in
long procession, praising God that they may now repair
to their church, and giving benison to the knight through
whom they are free to repair thither."

Meanwhile King Arthur and Gawain, "in sore misgiv-
ing for Lancelot, "have reached an assembly of knights
that is being held to win the Golden Circlet, owned

formerly by Perceval when he slew the Knight of the Fiery Dragon. They tarry to take part in it.

The first day of the journey King Arthur and Gawain are adjudged to have done best; but the second day one of the damsels of the tent reminds Gawain of a covenant he had made when journeying to visit the sick King Fisherman.

At the entrance to King Fisherman's kingdom a priest had told Gawain:

"Sir, you may not enter the castle save you bring the sword wherewith S. John was beheaded. But so you conquer the sword for us, this entrance will be free to you, and then will it be well known that you are worthy to behold the Holy Graal."

On his way to Albanie, the country of King Gurgalain, where this sword was kept, Gawain promised the King of Wales to show him the sword on his return journey. He found King Gurgalain distraught with grief, for a giant had carried off his son; if Gawain could bring him back his son, he pledged his word that he should have the sword.

Gawain tracked down the giant, whom he fought and killed, but not before the giant had slain the little prince. Bearing the dead child and the giant's head Gawain returned to King Gurgalain, who not only gave him the promised sword but also himself became a Christian.

On his return journey Gawain redeemed his promise to show the sword to the King of Wales, who, instead of giving it back to Gawain, placed it in his own treasury, only yielding it up on condition that Gawain would grant the first request made by a damsel, whatever that request might be.

When Gawain had again reached King Fisherman's

kingdom, he confessed his sins to a hermit,who warned him.

"Forget not to ask that which the other knight forgot."

And when, in King Fisherman's rich chamber, he gave him the sword, the King, after thanking him, also begged.

"I pray you for God's sake, hold me in remembrance tonight and forget not to speak the word."

As Gawain sat at meat that night with twelve ancient knights, each a hundred years old" and yet none of them seemed as though he were forty", two damsels entered the hall, one bearing the most holy Graal, and the other the lance.

"So sweet a smell and so holy came to them therefrom that they forgot to eat. So great a joy cometh to Gawain that nought remembereth he in his thinking save of God only. The knights are all daunted and sorrowful in their hearts, and look at Messire Gawain."

A second time the damsels bring in the Graal. This time Gawain sees a child in the midst of it. The Master of the Knights beckons to him; but again he speaks no word.

A third time the damsels bring in the Graal, and above it Gawain sees a "a King crowned, nailed upon a rood, and the spear still fast in his side. He hath great pity thereof, and of nought doth he remember him save of the pain that this King suffereth. The Master of the Knight summoneth him by word of mouth, but Messire Gawain is silent, as he that heareth not the knight speak."

And next morning Gawain leaves the Graal Castle, sorely discomfited.

And now, on the second journey to the Graal Castle, he is asked to redeem the pledge he had given to the King of Wales on that first one – that the first request made to him by a damsel should be granted, whatever that request might be.

The request is that "today you shall be he that doth worst of all the knights of the assembly, and that you bear none other arms save your own only, so that you shall be known of all them that are here present."

Gawain complies, "though sore it irked him, sith thus must he lose worship." And, indeed, "in great shame and dishonour was he held, and the knights said that never had they seen so craven a knight." Even King Arthur, who knew all the circumstances, commented:

"Never thought I that so good a knight might ever have known so well how to counterfeit such a bad one."

But on the third day Gawain acquits himself so superlatively well that he wins the Golden Circlet.

King Arthur and Gawain, continuing their journey, arrive at the Waste Manor, whose lady recognises them and holds them prisoner out of her hatred for Lancelot, who has slain her brother. They break out of their prison, and are received by the seven knights guarding the bridge "on the points of their lances."

Lancelot, coming hotfoot from the no-longer-waste Waste City in his attempt to overtake them, turns the melée in their favour. They have taken part of the karma of Lancelot's slaying of the lady's brother on themselves; when Lancelot has himself to face that karma, a quite new note is sounded.

The three ride on together, and come to a second assembly of knights. The prize of the tournament is the golden crown of a Queen who has just died, which carried with it the guardianship of her kingdom.

King Arthur wins the crown. The knight who had brought it tells him:

"Sir, you may now defend the land of the best earthly Queen who is dead, and whether the King be alive or dead none knoweth."

The King asks:

"Whose was the land? And what was the name of the Queen?"

The knight tells him:

"Sir, the king's name was Arthur, and the best king in the world was he; but in his kingdom the more part say that he is dead. And this crown was the crown of Queen Guenievre, that is dead and buried, whereof is sore sorrow. Briant of the Isles and my Lord Kay with him are burning the land; there is great war toward. The knights that may not leave Cardoil sent me to go among the assemblies of knights, that so I might hear tidings of my Lord King Arthur and my lords Gawain and Lancelot, and, if so I might find him, tell them how the land hath fallen under this grevious sorrow."

Arthur mourned, holding the golden crown. Lancelot mourned, saying "between his teeth that now hath his joy come to an end. Gawain may not stint of making dole."

Lancelot offers to go back and defend the kingdom while the King completes his pilgrimage. Arthur accepts his offer. Lancelot had set out on the pilgrimage to the Grail; but it was not in his destiny to complete it.

So Lancelot again takes leave of Arthur and Gawain, and, coming in the evening to the Castle of Griffons, seeks harbourage there for the night in spite of the many heads of knights that are hanging from the gateway. The lord of this castle is a brother of the knight of the Waste Manor slain by Lancelot; a damsel in the castle recognises Lancelot, and reports to the lord that he is harbouring his deadly enemy.

The lord of the castle decides that next morning he will "smite off his enemy's head and hang it above all the other;" but his daughter sends a privy messenger to Lancelot to warn him of his danger and to tell him that there is a cavern beneath the castle which runs underground as far as the forest. It is guarded by a lion and two griffons, and she sends him a brachet (hound) with whom the griffons love to play; while they are thus playing, he can pass them unharmed. At daybreak his steed will be awaiting him at the cavern's exit in the orchard at the forest's edge.

Towards day break Lancelot enters the cavern: the two griffons, by the light of the fire which they themselves cast forth, "espy the brachet and make her the greatest cheer in the world. Lancelot passes beyond without gainsay." He fights and slays the lion, "cometh forth into the orchard beside the forest, and wipeth his sword on the freshness of the green grass."

The freshness of the green grass, the fruiting orchard, introduce a note unheard till now. The daughter of the lord of the Castle of Griffons renounces an eye for an eye; it is with good that she repays evil.

Lancelot mounts his waiting steed, and rides all day till he reaches Avalon. Here, in the chapel, beside the coffin which holds the head of her son, Queen Guenievre lies in a rich coffin with four tall wax tapers alight at its four corners.

And beside it all night Lancelot keeps vigil.

Meanwhile King Arthur and Gawain continue their journey and reach the Graal Castle; and "Perceval, that was therewithin, made right great joy of their coming."

To Perceval King Arthur presents not only the Golden circlet which Gawain had won at the first journey, but also Queen Guenievre's gold crown, which he himself had won at the second.

"When Perceval knew that she was dead, he lamented her right sweetly. The King sojourneth in the castle and is highly honoured, and beholdeth the richness and the lordship and the great abundance that is everywhere."

In King Arthur's bestowal on Perceval of Queen Guenievre's golden crown one can sense an archetypal gesture. Guenievre had been Moon to Arthur's Sun; it is silver, the metal of the moon, that connects man with the cosmos. When the Queen does not accompany the pilgrimage, the Arthurian Mysteries are already being loosened from their cosmic ties; when the Queen dies, these ties are loosened further. The Arthur stream becomes free to unite with the Grail stream.

It becomes equally free to take an alternative course. The Round Table, that reflection on earth of the Zodiac, had been the most precious wedding gift to Arthur from King Leodagrance, the father of Guenievre. At the news of her death, her kinsman

Madeglant of Oriande, sent to Arthur this ultimatum:
"I am your enemy in two manner of ways; for the
Round Table which you hold by wrong, sith that the
Queen is dead, and for the New Law that you
hold." Arthur, says Madeglant, may continue to hold
the Round Table only if he renounces his Christian
belief and also weds Queen Jandree, Madeglant's
infidel sister.

It is as if the Arthurian Mysteries stand at the parting
of the ways. They may cling to their past, but at the
cost of becoming decadent, as some other noble Mysteries had done by outliving their due time. Or they
may withdraw their forces from their outward
framework and, together with other esoteric streams,
await in a germinal condition the time of their rebirth.
In defying Madeglant, in uniting with the Grail Stream,
they made the latter choice.

One day, while King Arthur still "sojourneth in the
Graal Castle," he is at the castle windows and sees a
great procession coming from beyond the bridge; one
clad in white bears a great cross at their head, and each
of those who follow bears a small cross and lighted candle. Last of all came one with a bell. They are singing
with sweet voices.

King Arthur cried:

"Ah, God, what folk be these?"

Percival told him:

"Sir, they are the hermits of this forest, that come to
chant before the Holy Graal within yonder chapel three
days in the week,."

King Arthur, with Perceval and Gawain, goes to meet

them; together they accompany the hermits into the chapel.

They took the bell from the last, and smote thereon at the altar; and then began they the service, most holy and most glorious. The Graal appeared at the sacring of the mass, in five several manners that none ought not to tell, for the secret things of the sacrament ought none to tell openly but he to whom God hath given it. King Arthur held all the changes, the last whereof was the change into the chalice."

We are told that King Arthur, on his return, introduces the chalice into his own kingdom which had known no chalice till then. This would seem to be saying, in an image, that the blood Christ shed on Golgotha had become a redemptive reality for the Arthur Mysteries, which had hitherto known and served Him as the Spirit of the Sun but had not known Him, as the Grail Mysteries had done, as the Spirit of the Earth.

In *Perceval li Gallois*, then, contrary to some other versions of the legend, but in harmony, surely, with what Rudolf Steiner tells us of the uniting of the two streams, King Arthur does himself achieve the Grail.

This is the solemn climax of the story. When tidings are brought to the Graal Castle that Aristot of Maraine has carried off Perceval's sister Dinrane from their mother's castle in the Valleys of Camelot, Perceval leaves to rescue her, and King Arthur and Gawain return to Cardoil, to share with Lancelot the burden of the war with Briant, Kay and Guenievre's kinsman, Madeglant. While the Arthurian Kingdom perishes in a long, tragic and disintegrating war, the Graal Castle falls slowly and gently away into an outer ruin pervaded by an atmosphere of such holiness that it makes saints of all who enter it. But in the spiritual worlds the essences of the Arthurian Mysteries and the Grail Mysteries await their recall together.

This, then is a thirteenth-century trouvère's imaginative picture of the meeting of the Arthur stream and the Grail stream in the year 869 A.D. of which Rudolf Steiner tells us.

This year, 869 A.D., is a momentous one. In it happenings in both sensible and supersensible worlds interreact to make it a crucial turning-point in mankind's history.

The Age of the Consciousness Soul does not dawn till the fifteenth century. But it is "signalised", Dr.Steiner tells us, by the ninth, and above all by the year 869 A.D. It is in this ninth century that Latin floods Europe, accelerating the withering of heart-wisdom into head-knowledge, so that the profounder significances of Christianity are no longer understood. By the middle of the century it was felt by the Roman Church Fathers that the intellect, which was increasingly "storming into evolution" and becoming increasingly incapable of spiritualised thinking, made esotericism a danger for some centuries to come.

Therefore Pope Nicholas I, who occupied the papal throne from 858 to 867 A.D., decided that henceforward supersensible truths were no longer to be a matter of living experience of the spiritual worlds, but of dogma, of faith alone.

So alongside this outer stream of historical Christianity,

the Grail and the Arthur streams, sheltered by the
wings of the Celtic Archangel, flowed as an esoteric and
for the most part invisible current, though from time to
time, says Rudolf Steiner, in "mysterious, repeated
glimpses of the Holy Grail or its secular reflection and
counterpart, the Round Table of King Arthur, men did
still feel the presence of something connected with vision of worlds beyond the earth, with living experience of
these worlds."

The meeting of the Arthur and Grail stream "over
Europe" in 869 A.D. was one of three destiny-fraught
meetings which happened in that year, and whose consequences still reverberate on into our own times.

Above, in the light streaming upward from this Grail-
Arthur meeting, a conference took place in the spiritual
worlds as to the shaping of evolution in preparation for
the new Michael Age which would begin on earth in
1879.

At this heavenly conference, Aristotle, Alexander and
many knights of the Round Table strove so to shape this
preparation that Christian impulses should pre-
dominate; over against them, Haroun el Raschid and
his counsellor strove as strongly in the cause of Arabism. The latter prevailed, and, as a consequence,
human evolution on earth in the following centuries
plunged even deeper into intellectualism.

But as a result of this decision, in the knights of the
Round Table who took part in this conference their
Cosmic Christianity lived yet more strongly, laid up as
a seed in preparation for that time when Michael
should again rule on the earth,

As the Arthur-Grail meeting over Europe had sent up
its light onto that conference in heaven, so the latter sent
down its shadow into the third meeting, held on earth.

At the eighth Ecumenical Council, held at Constantinople in 869 A.D., the Church Fathers outlawed spirit from the definition of man; it was henceforward heresy to believe him to be other than a being of body and soul with certain spiritual qualities. So was opened the way for men's achievement of ego-consciousness in complete freedom, but at the same time for the rapidly strenghening earthly intellect to gain further sway.

But from beneath the sheltering wing of the Celtic Archangel, in hidden ways the Arthur stream and the Grail stream still worked on.

In the twelfth century they hovered over the School of Chartres. "In a remarkable way" says Steiner, "this School of Chartres stands midway between the Arthur-principle and the Grail-principle, whose supersensible, invisible impulses made their way, not so much into the actual content of the teachings, as into the whole attitude and mood-of-soul of the pupils."

In the same century, also, with the founding of the Knights Templars in 1118, the forces of the Grail streamed into the new Order, with its esoteric aim of establishing the Holy Land as a centre free from Rome. These forces streamed also into certain "heretical" sects, such as the Cathars and the Albigenses, whose Christianity held esoteric reverberations. And in this same twelfth century, the esoteric Arthur stream and Grail stream emerged into exoteric romances, which troubadour and minnesinger carried from castle to castle across Europe.

The thirteenth and fourteenth centuries were a kind of spiritual Ice Age. The Transubstantiation was made dogma at the Lateral Council of 1215; the partaker was no longer permitted to perceive the pure Archetype of man in this "Third Movement" of the four-fold Mass.

In 1244, with the taking of Mount Ségur, their last stronghold, the Cathars were wiped out by the Roman Church's Crusade against them. In 1314 the Templars were wiped out by the miser-king, Philip le Bel, but with the Pope's connivance.

The way into the spiritual world seemed firmly closed. But the Grail stream which had flowed into the Knights Templars now flowed on further into Rosicrucianism. So, at first only among "cave-dwellers of the soul," the principle and practice of Christian Initiation were preserved without interruption.

With the dawn of our own epoch in 1413, the modern consciousness, built upon sense impressions, became paramount. Haroun el Raschid, reincarnating in the sixteenth century as that Father of Natural Science, Lord Bacon, and his former counsellor Amos Comenius, bring back their Arabism in transmuted forms, so that here on earth materialism, sense-restricted natural science and brain-bound thinking flourish.

But meanwhile, above in the spiritual worlds, in this same sixteenth century, Michael holds a great supersensible school in preparation for his own coming leadership on earth from 1879. Not only multitudes of spiritual beings take part on this, not only multitudes of elemental beings, but also multitudes of discarnate human beings on their way down to a new incarnation.

And the substance of Michael's teaching is that esoteric Christianity which in our time is to begin to come into its own again among men upon the earth – that Cosmic Christianity which combines the Arthurian experience of Christ as a Sun-Being in the aura of the Earth with the Grail experience of Him as the whole meaning of the Earth, born in the hearts of men.

We live today in that new Michael Age which began in 1879, and for which the great supersensible school of the sixteenth century had been a preparation – that school among whose pupils we ourselves may well have been.

Man has delved deep into the intellect. Now the time is ripe for him to rise again from intellectual to imaginative thinking, bearing with him the gifts he has wrested from the intellect – clarity and clear consciousness.

Kali Yuga, the great Dark Age, ended in 1899. With the turn of the century a new Light Age began. At the turn of the century Rudolf Steiner brought us Anthroposophy.

In Anthroposophy is one of the renewals of Cosmic Christianity, of that stream that ran through the Grail Quest and through the Round Table, through the Cathars, the Templars, the Rosicrucians – a stream which runs now underground, now above-ground, and which changes its outer form from century to century, according to human needs. The Celtic Cross with its sun-circle is metamorphosed into the Rose-Cross with its circle of seven red roses; the Grail cup and bleeding lance approach us in a new manifestation in the Rosicrucian meditation on the rose with its pure sap innocent of the passions colouring our own red blood.

When we ponder the legends of King Arthur and of the Grail, we are placing before our hearts in picture-form esoteric spiritual realities which long to come to a new birth in us.

LECTURES by RUDOLF STEINER:

Karmic Relationships, Vol. 8
 Torquay, 12-21 Aug. 1924. (R. Steiner Press).

Karmic Relationships,
 Vols. 1-4, Dornach, 16 Feb.-28 Sept. 1924.
 (R. Steiner Press).

Supersensible Influences in the History of Mankind,
 Dornach, 22 Sept.-1 Oct. 1922.

A Picture of Earth Evolution in the Future,
 Dornach, 13 May 1921, in "Golden Blade" 1960,
 and in "Materialism and the Task of Anthroposophy",
 (Anthroposophic Press).

CHAPTER IV

PERCEVAL'S SISTER AND THE DESCENT INTO HELL

*U**ne moulte trés cointe pucièle, Blanc com flours en may novele*" – thus does Gautier characterise Perceval's sister. In both *Perceval li Gallois* and *Le Morte d'Arthur* she plays a part which seems small but which spiritually is great. In both she reaches a stage along the mystical path of the Imitation of Christ achieved by no other woman in Grail and Arthurian romance.

In *Perceival li Gallois* she is introduced by a casual remark – Perceval had one sister, hight Dindrane. "We are told that Joseph of Arimathea was uncle to their mother (called always "the Widow Lady"), who had three brothers – the rich King Fisherman of the Graal Castle, the Hermit-King Pelles of the Lower Folk, and the King of Castle Mortal," in whom there was as much bad as there was good in the other twain."

"He that was head of the lineage on the father's side was named Nicodemus." Thus both in Perceval and in Dindrane are united the streams flowing from the two who together took down Christ's Body from the Cross. In Dindrane, as we shall see, this united heritage works with especial power and grace.

When Perceval was still "a right young squire," he had, to his own astonishment, slain with his javelin the Red knight who was Lord of Shadows. Perceval left his home in the Valleys of Camelot, went to the Court of King Arthur to be knighted, then "departed to seek adventure in other kingdoms."

"Thereof did sore trouble come thereafter." For Chaos the Red, the brother of the slain knight, swore to avenge his death, and made war on the Widow Lady.

One by one he reft her castles from her, till, when Perceval had been seven years absent, she had only Camelot left. And even Camelot, since she now had only five ancient knights left to defend her, her persecutors already regarded as their own.

("Lords, think not that it is this Camelot whereof these tellers of tales do tell their tales, there where King Arthur so often held his court. This Camelot that was the Widow Lady's stood upon the uttermost headland of the wildest isle of Wales by the sea to the West. Nought was there save the hold and the forest and the waters that were round about it. The other Camelot, of King Arthur's, was peopled of folk and was seated at the head of the King's land, at the entrance of the kingdom of Logres.")

It is at this point in the romance that a stranger knight finds his way to Camelot by the sea to the West, to crave harbourage for the night. And it is at this point that Dindrane enters upon that path of dedication, ever unwearied, ever deepening, ever more fervent, ever more anguished, which leads her "among darkling rocks and through forests right deep and perilous," into the very maw of Hell itself.

At the Widow Lady's Camelot "there was, between the hold and the forest, a small chapel that stood upon four columns of marble, and before the altar a right fair coffin."

When Perceval had been a child, he had asked his father, Alain le Gros, who lay in that coffin.

His father had replied:

"Fair son, never have I heard tell of none that might know, save only the letter on the coffin say that when the Best Knight in the world shall come hither, it will open, and then it will be seen who lieth therein."

Now the Widow Lady was convinced by the reasoning of a mother's heart (and events were to prove her right) that it was Perceval's destiny to become this Best Knight in the world. So when, on the day on which Perceval had been seven years absent, she and Dindrane came over the castle bridge and saw a knight reining-in his steed to gaze at the coffin, she was overcome with joy.

"Now haste," she cried to Dindrane, "to see whether it is he!"

But when they reached the tomb, and found it still fast, the Widow Lady broke into loud lamentation.

"Sir," said Dindrane to the knight, "welcome may you be! My mother weeps because she had supposed you to be her son."

"Sir," said the Widow Lady,"what is your name?"

"Lady," said he, "I am called Gawain, King Arthur's nephew."

Then gladly they brought him into Camelot, to lodge with them that night.

When they have eaten together, Dindrane falls at Gawain's feet, telling him that Chaos the Red and the Lord of the Moors are holding a tourney on the morrow, "and he who shall do best shall hold this castle for his own for a year and a day, for you will understand that it is no more my lady mother's sith these knights say it is theirs."

She begs Gawain to take part in the tourney. This he does, and is adjudged victor. So Camelot is "stablished in peace again" for a year and a day. "No need to wonder whether Messire Gawain was well harboured that night at the castle."

Having set all there in order, Gawain goes on his way; and the truce is drawing towards its end when, on coming to the Graal Castle, he meets Dindrane a second time.

She has come to her uncle, the languishing King Fisherman, in search of tidings of Perceval, "for the war will soon be resumed against us, and God succour us not if we find not my brother whom we have lost so long."

But since he cast his uncle into languishment by omitting to ask whom the Graal serveth, Perceval has not been heard of there. "And good reward of harbouring him." King Fisherman comments drily, "had I not."

So now Dindrane "goeth seeking for Perceval by all the kingdoms and strange counties in sore misease, nor may she find any to tell her tidings of him."

And Perceval, on his part, remains unconscious of his mother's plight till he comes to one of her castles, called the Key of Wales ("for that it is the gateway of that land"), and finds it in the hands of Chaos the Red. Him he slays, "right full of anguish of heart for that this knight had warred upon his mother and had reft her of his castle.

Ordering the castle to be delivered up to his mother, Perceval departs, and, meeting a damsel with a car drawn by three white harts, learns further:

"Your sister goeth in quest of you; for never had your mother so sore need of help as now she hath; nor never again shall your sister have joy at heart until such time as she shall have found you."

This damsel with the Car (in which are the heads of a hundred and fifty knights slain because Perceval had "demanded not whom one serveth of the Graal") has already visited King Arthur's Court and left there a brachet (a hound) and a shield "banded argent and azure, with a red cross and a boss of gold," in keeping for a knight who shall come for them, and who will leave in exchange a shield "of sinople,with a white hart."

Soon afterwards, Dindrane in her searching, also comes to King Arthur's Court, only once more to find neither Perceval or any tidings of him. The brachet, "who had never rejoiced since he was brought into the hall, maketh great joy of her than ever was brachet seen to make before." And when Dindrane sees the waiting shield, she recognises it for the Graal shield of prophecy, to be borne only by the Best Knight in the world. So she begs the King that when this knight shall come, he shall be sent, in default of Perceval, to succour her mother at Camelot.

But alas, the knight – Perceval himself – comes by dead of night. He takes the brachet and the shield and leaves behind the shield with the white hart. Dindrane, "no whit joyful" next morning to find the Best Knight in the world has come and gone without hearing of her petition, departs in haste to seek him.

No sooner has she done so than Gawain and Lancelot arrive at King Arthur's Court. Lancelot, having fought with its owner, recognises the shield of the white hart.

"Now know I well that Perceval hath been here, for this shield was he wont to bear. So nigh did I see it that methought he would have killed me!"

"'Lords,' saith the King, 'I am bound to beseech his aid on behalf of a damsel.'

"'Sore discounselled is she,' saith the Queen. 'She hath told me that she was daughter of Alain li Gros of the Valley of Camelot, and that her name is Dindrane.'

"'Ha, Lady,' saith Messire Gawain, 'She is sister to the knight that hathe borne away the shield. I will go in quest of him.'

"'And I,' saith Lancelot. 'Sir, we will tell him his sister seeks him, and that she hath been at your Court.'

"The two knights depart from the Court, and leave that castle far behind them, and ride in the midst of a high forest until they find a cross there where all the roads of the forest join together.'

And here they part, "that we may the sooner have tidings."

Three times Gawain finds Perceval without knowing him. The fourth times Joseus, the young hermit who is Perceval's cousin, tells each who the other is, "whereof both make themselves right joyous.'

Gawain tells Perceval:

"Your sister was at Court, and besought the help of the knight that should bear away the shield. She asked your aid as she that deemed not you were her brother. The King sent us forth in quest of you, myself and Lancelot. For your father is dead, and your mother, if you succour her not shortly, must needs become a beggar, for of the fifteen castles she wont to have in your father's time, she hath now only Camelot."

"Then Perceval saith that never will he rest again until he shall have found his sister and his mother."

And so they part.

First, Perceval comes to the chapel where a hermit is singing the Mass of the Dead for Lohot, King Arthur's son." On the morrow he rideth through the forest and he that would right gladly hear tidings of his mother, nor never before hath he been so desirous thereof as he is now.

"He heard, at the right hour of noon, a damsel under a tree, that prayed right sweetly the Saviour of the World for succour. For needs she must go to the most perilous place that is in the world and save she might bring someone someway with her, never would that she had to do be done."

The damsel cried:

"Unhappy am I that I have gone through all the lands of Great Britain, yet may I hear no tidings of my brother. Either he is dead, or he is in lands so far away, none may hear tidings of him. Ah, sweet Lady, aid us when we may have no aid of any other."

Then Perceval rode forward, and she looked and saw the shield about his neck, with its red cross and its boss of gold. And she knew it for the shield destined for the Best Knight in the world.

She ran to meet him, and held his stirrup, and would have kissed his foot.

She cried:

"Sir, have pity of my mother and of me. For, if your aid fail us, we know not where to turn. Had you been my brother, whom I cannot find, I might have called upon you to a greater right. Sir, do you remember you of the brachet that went away with you? He would never make joy nor know any save me alone. By this know I well that if you knew the soreness of our need you would succour us."

Perceval replied:

"Damsel, King Arthur sent for me by the two best knights of his Court. And so much will I do herein as that God and he shall be well pleased thereof."

Now Dindrane knew great joy, though she did not know her brother. Perceval knew she was his sister, but did not reveal himself.

She mounted her mule with his help; and as they rode on, side by side, she told him that that night she must go into the Graveyard Perilous, and she must go in alone. For she had learnt from a hermit that the Lord of the Moors could only be overcome with the help of a portion of the altar-cloth in the graveyard chapel.

"The cloth is of the most holiest, for our Lord God was covered therewith in the Holy Sepulchre; and may God save my life this night, for the place is sore perilous.

"Sir, go your way to towards the castle of Camelot. See, this is my way, that is but little frequented, and that no knight durst tread without dread. Our Lord God have your body in keeping; for mine own this night shall be in sore jeopardy."

So they parted.

Dindrane rode on alone through the deep forest. The sun had set and night fallen when she came to the great crucifix which guarded the entrance to the graveyard.

She "entered in all alone, and found great multitude of tombs; nor none need wonder whether she had shuddering and fear, for such a place must needs be dreadful to a lonely damsel, there where lay so many knights that had seen slain in arms in the forest.

"Within the graveyard might no evil spirit meddle; but never might no hermit remain within for the evil spirits that appeared each night all round about, that took the shapes of the knights that lay dead still in the forest."

Dindrane sees these evil spirits now, surrounding the graveyard in the shape of knights, all black, fighting and gashing each other with swords of fire; their clashing and clamour and uproar sounded and resounded throughout the forest.

"Such affright hath she thereof that she nigh fell to the ground in a swoon. The mule whereon she sate draweth wide his nostrils, and goeth in much fear. She signeth herself of the cross."

She sees before her the chapel, small and ancient. She alights and enters "a great brightness of light."

"She seeth above the altar the most holy cloth for the which she was come thither, that was right ancient, and a smell came thereof so sweet and glorious that no sweetness of the world might equal it. She cometh towards the altar, thinking to take the cloth, but it goeth up into the air as if the wind had lifted it."

Then Dindrane cried:

"Fair Father God, the good knight Joseph took you in his arms beside the rood, and laid your Body in the holy sepulchre, wherein were you covered of the sovran cloth for the which have I come in hither.

"Grant it be your pleasure that I may have it, for love of the knight by whom it was set in this chapel; sith that I am of his lineage, it ought well to manifest itself in this sore need, so it come according to your pleasure."

The cloth descended, and Dindrane found a portion of it separated off. This she took and kissed, "and set it near herself full worshipfully. Never did none enter into the chapel that might touch the cloth save only this one damsel."

Without, the forest still rang with the uproar of the evil spirits, and the graveyard was ringed with fire by their

flaming swords. At the stroke of midnight a Voice spoke
from about the Chapel:
"King Fisherman is dead. And now hath the King of
Castle Mortal seized his castle; and never since hath the
Graal appeared. And you, damsel, that are within, suc-
coured may you never be, save of your brother only."
Then a wailing went up from the graveyard, and from
the evil spirits that encompassed it a groaning, and at
their departing the earth trembled.
Dindrane was in sore dismay, hearing that only her
brother could succour her; "and at her uncle's death
had she right sore sorrow. She was in the chapel until it
was day, and then commended herself to God and
mounted on her mule and issued forth of the graveyard
full speed."

Dindrane had reached the Valleys of Camelot before
she overtook Perceval. She told him of King Fisherman's death, and of how the King of Castle Mortal had
seized the Graal Castle, and of how she had been told
that only her brother's help could avail her.
"Perceval is silent, and hath great pity in his heart."
From the windows of the castle the Widow Lady sees
them coming, and cries:
"God grant this may be my son!"
And she hastens out to meet them.
Perceval and Dindrane have alighted at the tomb
beneath the four columns of marble between the hold
and the forest. As Perceval touches the tomb, the
Widow Lady sees it open, and Dindrane fall at his feet
in joy.
"Then knew the Widow lady that it was her son; and

she ran to him, and kissed him, and began to make the greatest joy that ever lady made."

Beside him who lay in the tomb there were letters sealed with gold. The Widow Lady sent for her chaplain, and bade him open them and read them.

He told her:

"These letters witness of him who lieth here that he was one of them, that helped to un-nail Our Lord from the Cross."

"Before the sepulchre closed again, they looked in beside him, and found the pincers all bloody wherewith the nails had been drawn."

Before Perceval rides out to meet the Lord of the Moors in combat, Dindrane gives him the pieces of the altar-cloth from the Chapel in the Graveyard Perilous, "whereof a holy hermit told me that never should our land be conquered back until such time as you should have hereof."

Perceval reverently kisses it, touches his eyes and face with it then "goeth out of the gateway like a lion unchained."

He brings back his adversary a prisoner, and presents him to the Widow lady, saying:

"Lady see here the Lord of the Moors! Well might you expect him eftsoons, sith that you were to have yielded up to him your castle the day after tomorrow."

So terrible was the retribution visited upon the Lord of the Moors that his people brought to Perceval "the keys of all the castles that had been reft of his mother; and all the knights that had before renounced their allegiance returned thereto."

One day, as the Widow Lady sat at meat, Perceval seated beside Dindrane,"behold you, the Damsel of the Car came in."

She said to Perceval:

"King Hermit, your mother's brother, sendeth you word that, as you come not with haste into the land that was King Fisherman's, the New Law that God hath established will be brought low. For the King of Castle Mortal, that hath seized the land and castle, hath made be cried throughout all the country how all they that would fain maintain the Old Law shall have protection of him."

Then Perceval departed from his mother, "with her good will and the good will of his sister." After slaying the Knight of the Fiery Dragon, he wins back the Graal Castle from the King of Castle Mortal, who slays himself on the battlements.

King Arthur comes on pilgrimage to the Graal Castle, and is sitting at meat with Perceval when the Damsel of the Car brings the latter dire news;

"Sir, Aristot of Moraine, that is cousin to the Lord of the Moors that you slew, warreth upon your mother, and hath carried off your sister by force into the castle of a vavasour of his, and saith that he will take her to wife and will have all her land that your mother ought to hold of right.

"Never had knight custom so cruel as he, for when he hath espoused any damsel, he cuts of her head with his own hand, then seeketh another to slay in like manner."

Perceval sets out for "the castle of Ariste, whereof Aristot is Lord, "On the way he comes to the hermitage of his uncle, King Hermit, who had formerly been King Pelles of the Lower Folk. There he finds a damsel laying out the body of King Hermit, and hears that Aristot had slain him suddenly after mass, "on account of his nephew, Perceval, whom he loveth not."

Perceval departs "as he that hath great desire to take vengeance," and, confronting Aristot, announces:

"I am come to my sisters wedding; of right it ought not be made without me."

Perceval slays Aristot in single combat, and brings his head to Dindrane in the vavasours's castle, with the greeting:

"Weep not, for your wedding has failed. You may know it well by this token."

He escorts her back to Camelot and restores her to their mother, then "took his leave, for he had not yet achieved all that he had to do."

Dindrane and the Widow Lady "remained long time at Camelot, and led a good life and a holy," till the Damsel with the Car came to bring them to Perceval in "his most holy castle."

With them they brought to the Graal Castle the altar-cloth from the Graveyard Perilous,"and presented it there where the Graal was." They brought also the body from the tomb before the Castle of Camelot, and placed it in the Graal Chapel; and beside it Perceval caused to be placed the body "of the other knight that was before the entrance of the Graal Castle."

So Joseph of Arimathea and Nicodemus, who together had taken down Christ's body from the Cross and laid it in the sepulchre, now shared one grave before the altar of the Graal. One is reminded of the Three Kings, making room for one another in one grave as each after each they died and came to be buried.

And, in the Graal Castle, Perceval, with his mother and his sister, lived "a holy life and a religious, till first the Widow Lady, then Dindrane, also, passed way, and a ship came, "with a white sail and a red cross thereon" and fair companies of angels, to carry Perceval to the Island of the Master.

Legend tells us that not only did Joseph of Arimathea lay the body of Christ in his own tomb, but that he laid it there wrapped in a very special shroud.

This is the story of the shroud as told in the Middle Ages:

Syndonia was a maiden with great skill in weaving; at the death of her father, she and her mother fell into great poverty, and her mother bade her to take some of her work to the market in Arimathea, to sell to buy them bread.

"Syndonia answered:

"Mother, your will shall be done. I have a cloth here that fell so graciously to work that it is more curious than I have skill of of myself.'

"Let me see the cloth," said the lady.

And when she saw it, she said:

"Blessed be the the Lord that made thee to work such a cloth, my daughter. Sell it to no man till he shall tell thee what he will do with it.'

Then Syndonia washed herself and arrayed her to the market. And in the market stood Joseph of Arimathea, searching for a precious cloth to buy for to wrap our Lord Jesu in. When he saw the cloth which hanged on the maid's arm he asked her if she would sell it. And she answered she would. Then he asked her the

price and she said thirty bezants. And Joseph paid to her thirty bezants.Then she prayed him that he would tell her what he would do with it, and he answered:
"Daughter, this day is dead a holy man that men called Jesus of Nazareth, and Him I purpose for to bury and wind in this cloth. Tell me now who made this cloth."
And she said that herself had made it.
And Joseph asked her what was her name, and she said:
"Syndonia, sir."
Then said Joseph:
"Now after you I shall name this cloth, for this cloth shall be called Syndonia."

And, indeed, so it was.
An early French History of the Holy Grail tells how, when Christ rose, He came to Joseph of Arimathea in prison, bringing to him the Grail. He said:
"In your care do I leave this image of My death. The vessel in which my body is consecrated in the form of the Host, shall point to the grave in which you laid Me; the paten laid upon it, to the stone before its mouth; the cloth covering the wine shall be called the corporal, as a remembrance of the napkin wherewith you covered Me. So the image of your deed will be for ever before men."
But though the cloth covering the Elements was indeed known as the corporal, among the folk it was known as the sidonia or the sedony.
This simple little legend of Syndonia is full of implicit undertones.
Her father is dead – she, like Perceval and Dindrane, is the child of a widow. This was a term in use in some of the Mysteries for a soul undergoing initiation. King

Hiram of Tyre, for example, who could build the Temple Solomon could not, was the son of a widow.

Then, too, Syndonia is conscious that the shroud's weaving excels her own skill. Rudolf Steiner tells us that the ancient Celts were well aware, when they created things of especial beauty, that they had received help from spiritual beings. There is perhaps an echo of this in the story – again Celtic – of two chapels in Brittany with specially beautiful frescoes, that angels had flown to and fro between them, bearing the artists' tools from each to other. Is it not the most likely thing in the world that angels should beautify the shroud that was to enfold the body which for three years has housed the Spirit of the Sun?

Joseph gave Syndonia thirty bezants for the shroud. The bezant was a golden coin. Can we perhaps see in the purchase price of the shroud a kind of redemption of Judas' thirty pieces of silver? For Judas' purchase price was moon-money, received for betrayal, in darkness, both of the night-time and of his own soul. The gold of the thirty bezants belonged both to the sun and to the Sun. The shroud they purchased was to be the sheath enfolding the being of the Sun while, in the depths of the Earth, he recreated Man.

The bezant carries with it an overtone of the esoteric wisdom of the Eastern church, for it is said to have been first coined in Byzantium – hence its name. Here in England it carries an overtone of eucharistic use, for it was formerly the King's offering at the sacrament. This whole solemn transaction of the buying of the shroud is full of delicate intimations of spiritual currents weaving invisibly in the background.

Joseph provided the shroud; Nicodemus provided the myrrh within the shroud. This, quickening the volatilis-

ing of the material elements of the Body, actually
assisted in the re-birth of Archetypal Man.

Veronica's veil, the earliest of the Passion relics, is said
to bear the imprint of the face of Jesus of Nazareth from
her wiping of his brow on the way to Golgotha. So real
was this to the medieval church that the incident was
included in the Stations of the Cross. The French Grail
romance we have just quoted describes the healing of
Vespasian's leper-son by the mere sight of this holy
relic. The Holy Shroud is said similarly to have
received the imprint of the sacred Body. To what
spiritual truths does this point?

'The etheric body of man sets aside very fine, delicate
pictures of itself which weave on in the etheric environment. We are all the time surrounded by such copies;
but only under certain conditions can they be seen
clairvoyantly.

In a unique way the Body of Christ was able to separate
such etheric images from itself. Out of the pure will of
His devotion, etheric life-forces streamed forth from
Him. Veronica is a disciple able to keep such an image
in her soul and nurse it; healing forces could well be
passed on by such a disciple when met by the right sus-
ceptibility."

In the same way we can perhaps understand how a virgin soul of Dindrane's high courage and development
could draw on the virtue left by the powerful etheric
body of Jesus of Nazareth in the shroud which had witnessed incredible miracles in the darkness of the tomb.

Why is it that the Lord of the Moors cannot be overcome
without the aid of supersensible forces?

From the eighth to the thirteenth century, wave after wave of Moors invaded Spain, their culture spreading over the whole of Europe and influencing even its Christian monks. It was a clear-cut conflict between Christ's new Sun-Age and the untiring encroachments of Mahomet's moon-forces persisting long after their due time. Again and again we find the Old Law and the New Law specifically mentioned in the Grail and Arthurian romances – the Old Law of the pre-Christian monotheism, the New Law of the threefoldness of the Trinity.

As early as the sixth century, Arabism had produced a brilliant but already abstract culture. The dried-up intellect invaded Europe from this direction even before it began to manifest itself from within.

That Dindrane was carried off by Aristot, cousin to the Lord of the Moors whom Perceval had slain with the aid of the altar-cloth underlines this. For the teachings of Aristotle (in French, Artistot), translated into Arabic in the sixth century, were already materialised in this translation, through which they penetrated into European thought.

In *Perceval li Gallois*, Aristot, therefore appears in the ranks of the Moors. But there was another stream in European culture which, deriving its Aristotelianism direct from the Greek, received the life-forces filling his philosophy and regarded him as a preparer of Christianity.

So, over against the Moorish Aristot of *Perceval li Gallois* must be placed the Aristot found worthy of being carved on Chartres Cathedral – the true Aristotle who takes part in the heavenly conference on the side of Michael and the Arthurian knights, against Haroun el Raschid, out of whose culture was born a dark double for the great philosopher.

The Lord of the Moors, then, cannot be overcome without the aid of supersensible forces because this conflict is primarily one belonging to supersensible spheres – one that casts a tragic karmic shadow into later centuries in the over-intellectualising of the new spiritual consciousness due to be born in our own time.

Dindrane's journey to the Graveyard Perilous is taken to safeguard the Valleys of Camelot. Why is this so urgent that she puts her body, if not her soul, into jeopardy?

In *Perceval li Gallois*, Perceval's mother is invariably referred to as the Widow Lady. In Wolfram's *Parzival*, his mother, Herzeleide, is a widow. Chrétian de Troyes makes it clear in his opening sentence that his hero is undergoing Initiation – "In spring the son of the widow started out in the lonely wood."

"Perceval" is a Mystery name; it means "to go through, to pierce the valley." One cannot escape the conclusion that the Valleys of Camelot are concerned with a Mystery Centre, a place of initiation.

It is Celtic, a place withdrawn, "in uttermost Wales." Grail Christianity had its esoteric home in King Fisherman's Castle. In the Valleys of Camelot one sees a home, a haven, of Cosmic Christianity.

The two who took down Christ's Body from the Cross are buried apart – Joseph of Arimathea outside the Graal Castle, Nicodemus as a guardian of the Arthur stream.

When Grail stream and Arthur stream have experienced their first steps towards union, first in the person of Perceval, and then in the Arthurian pilgrimage, the Celtic initiation can gently pass away. Joseph and Nicodemus are re-buried side by side before the altar of the Graal. The two streams have come together, and with the deaths of the Widow Lady and of Dindrane will presently withdraw from outer but not from inner history.

Not only did Joseph and Nicodemus take down the Body from the Cross together. Not only did they both receive Christ's Blood. Not only did they together lay the Body in Joseph's grave. But with that which followed the laying in the grave – Holy Saturday's Descent into Hell – both are associated in the apocryphal Gospel of Nicodemus.

It is Joseph and Nicodemus who bring to the priests at Jerusalem the tidings of Christ's descent into Hell, of His harrowing of Hell, and of His release from Hell of souls long held in bondage. It is Joseph and Nicodemus who bring the priests to Arimathea, to meet the two sons of Simeon, newly risen from the dead. And when the two sons of Simeon have each written for the priests an independent account of the Light appearing in the Land of Shades, it is in the hands of Joseph and Nicodemus that they leave one copy of their record of this glorious miracle.[5]

It is in every way fitting that it should be Dindrane, in whom is united the lineage of them both, who makes the descent to the very gates of Hell to bring back the shroud Christ left there on His own descent.

Dindrane is a soul on that mystical path of the Imitation of Christ which in the Middle Ages was a path of

Christian initiation. Even Aristot's squires are "right sorrowful" for her when she is in his power, and say   that she "is one of most noble lineage and of great beauty and of the most worth in the world."

The first five of the seven stages of this path are clearly marked in her.

She has that universal humility which belongs to the first stage, the Washing of the Feet. Often, indeed, it is expressed literally in falling at the feet of those she meets, or attempting to kiss their feet.

The bearing of sorrows and sufferings with patience and courage which marks the second stage, the Scourging, we also find in her on a grand and heroic scale.

Her willingness to spend herself in the quest for someone else's good in the face of heart-breaking rebuffs from fate belongs to the third stage, the Crowning with Thorns.

To carry one's physical body through the world as merely an outer instrument, a mark of the fourth stage, the Bearing of the Cross, makes transparent that strange use of the word *body* when we would have expected *soul*. ("Our Lord God have your body in keeping; for mine own this night shall be in sore jeopardy.") In the fifth stage, the Mystic Death, one is encompassed by darkness, then, for a moment, with the rending asunder of the veil, one experiences evil – this is the Descent into Hell.

And this is, in fact, what happens at the Graveyard Perilous. She is surrounded by demons – she experiences evil in its prototypal form. Later, when she is carried off by Artisot, she meets the same experience in human metamorphosis.

Our own age of the Consciousness Soul is the time when man has more than ever to come face to face with evil. The Descent into Hell has a relevance for us even beyond its relevance in the Middle Ages. In the depth of her experience of this, Dindrane runs ahead in the vanguard of evolution.

Dindrane is a being who gives herself in love. Thomas à Kempis' noble passage on love sums up her story:

"Love carrieth a burden without a burden, and maketh everything that is bitter sweet and tasteful. Love complaineth not of impossibility. Love is watchful, and, sleeping, sleepeth not; being weary is not tired; being pressed is not straitened; but like a lively flame breaking upwards, it passeth securely through all. If anyone loveth, he knoweth what this voice cryeth."

REFERENCES
Gautier de Doulens' *Continuation* of Chrétien de Troyes' *Le Conte du Graal.*
Blackletter Gospel of Nicodemus, 1511, printed by Wynkin de Worde (In British Museum).
Le Petit Saint Graal, Sire Robert de Borron (thirteenth century).
Der Gral und seine Hüter, Meyer.
The Gospel of Nicodemus, Second Century.
The Imitation of Christ, Thomas à Kempis.

LECTURES by RUDOLF STEINER:

The Gospel of St. John and its Relation to the Other Gospels, (Cassel) 24 June-7July 1909. (Anthroposophic Press).

CHAPTER V

PERCIVALE'S SISTER AND THE SHIP OF SOLOMON
Le Morte d'Arthur

In *Perceval li Gallois* we experience with Perceval's sister birth-pangs and growing-pangs on the path of the Imitation of Christ. In *Le Morte d'Arthur*, Perceval's sister also treads this path, right to its transendant culmination of self-sacrifice. But we also find her fulfilling an exalted destiny as guide, guardian and instructress of Malory's three Grail heroes.

A Welsh Triad runs:

"The three knights of Arthur's Court who found the Grail – Galath (Galahad), Peredur (Percivale), Bort (Bors). All three were descended from the family of Joseph of Arimathea, and from the lineage of the Prophet David."

The Mystery-teaching which prepares these three knights for the finding of the Grail they receive from Percivale's sister. She is the King's daughter, a maiden holy, calm and wise, deeply versed in matters of the spirit. We may think of her as the hierophant in particular of Galahad's initiation.

This achievement of the Grail by these three knights is foretold by Percivale's aunt even before the young men have unfolded their fellowship. She, who "had once been Queen of the Waste Lands, Queen of most riches in the world," was now a recluse, dwelling in "a priory place, whose chapel had a window, that she might see up to the altar."

When Percivale visits her there, she tells him of Merlin's prophecy that there would be "three white bulls" who would achieve the Sancgreal, and that one of them would surpass all other knights. She adds that this knight was that Sir Galahad who had "sat at his meat in the Siege Perilous upon Whit Sunday last past."

Her words fire Percivale to resolve to seek Galahad's friendship. "For God's love, fair aunt, can you teach me some way where I may find him, for much would I love the fellowship of him?" But there is no need for human manipulation. Destiny has the matter firmly in hand.

Galahad, asleep one night in a hermitage, is awakened by a gentlewoman. She tells him:

"I will that ye arm you, and, mount upon your horse, and follow me; for I will show you within these three days the highest adventure that ever any knight saw."

She conducts him to a castle, "and there had he great cheer, for the lady of that castle was the damsel's lady." So, by dead of night, his initiation is put in train.

When Galahad has eaten and slept, they armed him by torchlight; then they rode through the night to a shore where a ship awaited them. In the ship were Bors and Percivale, who greeted him with joy:

"Sir Galahad, you be welcome. We have abidden you long."

Galahad and the lady of the castle enter the ship, and now it is revealed that she is daughter to King Pellinore, and therefore sister to Percivale, "who makes great joy of her."

The wind drove the ship through the night," and within a while it dawned."We are given to understand that this coming together of the four most deeply involved in Malory's Grail-quest is one which they experience while out of their physical bodies, upon the sea of the etheric world.

The ship drove between two rocks, "passing great and marvellous, and there was a whirlpool in the sea." We are reminded of Scylla and Charybdis, and of the perilous passage man must navigate between the Luciferic and Ahrimanic when he sets sail on a voyage of spiritual development.

Beyond the rocks they draw near to another ship, "marvellous fair and rich, with neither man nor woman therein. On the end of the ship is written a dreadful word and a marvellous: *Thou man that shalt enter this ship, beware thou be in steadfast belief; for I am Faith, and if thou fail I shall not help thee."*

The way of initiation may not be trodden lightly. Percivale's sister warns them that " this ship is so perfect, it will suffer no sin in it."

In the midst of the ship they found "a fair bed, and at its foot a marvellous sword." Percivale set his hand to it, but could not grip it. Bors set his hand to it, but also failed.

To Galahad Percivale's sister said:

"The drawing of the sword is warned to all men, save only unto you."

From the beginning she knows him to be the knight who shall most fully achieve the Sancgreal.

The girdle of the sword is "but poorly to account, and

not able to sustain such a rich sword." On the scabbard
of snakeskin is written in letters of gold:
"This girdle ought not to be done away but by the hands
of a maid, and she a King's and Queens's daughter; and
she must be a maid all the days of her life, both in will
and in work."
Above the bed's head there are six spindles – two as
white as snow; above these, two as red as blood; and two
above all, as green as emeralds.
Percivale's sister tells them, that these spindles were cut
from the tree "where Eve came to gather fruit." When
she left Paradise she took with her a bough from it. She
planted it, and from it grew a tree as white as snow.
When Abel was conceived beneath it, part of the tree
turned green. When, later Cain slew Abel beneath it, that
part of the tree turned red.

In these six spindles we recognise the three shoots of the
tree of Paradise enshrined in the wonderful medieval
Holy Legend of the Cross. The legend speaks of three
shoots; but Rudolf Steiner, in his revealing references to
it, speaks of two groups of three – the astral, etheric and
physical bodies, and Spirit-Self, Life-Spirit and
Spirit-man, into which it is man's task to transmute
them.
He says:
"In this legend we have to do with something connected
with the development of the human race. Three shoots
from the tree of Paradise – Atma, Manas, Buddhi –
grew together into the trinity which forms the basis of
all evolution, having been planted in the Earth by Seth,
that son of Adam who took the place of Abel. While the

Sons of Cain develop the sciences, the Sons of Seth cultivate the spiritual in man.

"Physical, etheric and astral bodies enwrap and ensheath the higher nature, the real spiritual Trinity, and are like an external image of the three higher forces. The Old Covenant had the task of making these three lower natures at home on the earth. During this whole time of the Old Covenant, the Sons of Cain were building the Temple, the outer covering of man. From the Tree of Paradise came what made the three external bodies living; this is symbolically expressed in this wood being later used for the Cross. Man's actual task in his earthly evolution was to raise a stage higher the three bodies he had received."

We can see the story of Lemurian man reflected in the three colours as Percivale's sister relates these to the successive stages of his Fall. Man's original physical body may be thought of as having had the purity of snow; an old legend tells us in a beautiful image that all the animals, too, in Paradise were white.

When Abel was conceived, it was in a quite new way, under the influence of the Moon-forces, instead of under those of the Sun, as Cain had been. The etheric forces take their rhythm from the moon; and in the world around us it is the plant world which most manifests the etheric. In the green of the plant world the etheric "shoot" is displayed.

When Cain slays Abel, the red of the roused blood and of the spilt blood is conjured up. Through the astral body the red blood rages till it is redeemed and transmuted.

The legend of the three shoots is preserved in a very living and beautiful form in the *Ordinalia*, the fourteenth century cycle of Cornish Mystery-Plays. Here they are

spoken of as growing originally into three wands, each
an ell high, one of cedar, one of cypress, one of pine.
By each successive early Hebrew initiate they are treas-
ured with joy and reverence.
Aaron say of them:

> "Blessed are these rods.
> From all the herbs of the world
> So sweet a fragrance
> Will come again never."

And Moses:

> "Grace is so great in them
> That I will wrap them,
> With every care
> In silk and fine linen."

God sends Gabriel to lead King David to Mount Tabor,
where Moses has planted them, and to bring them back
to Jerusalem. Here they root and unite and grow into
one tree.

David decrees:

> "Since God has planted them in this place,
> here shall they stay,
> And that this tree may have high honour,
> Let there be made a circlet of silver
> Each year to measure its girth."

Year by year, a new circle of silver is fastened about it.
It grows and flourishes, and David loves to rest beneath
it, for in its shadow creative impulses come to him.
Under this tree he writes his Psalms, and it is there that
the thought of building a Temple comes to him. But an
angel sitting on one of its boughs tells him that this is
the task of his son Solomon.

Solomon also loves to sit beneath the tree, and in its shadow that wisdom comes to him which he writes down in the books of Ecclesiastes, Proverbs and The Song of Solomon. When the tree has been growing for thirty years, Solomon's Temple is almost completed. He goes to inspect it, praises the masons and carpenters who have worked on it.

He asks them:

"But tell me, where shall we find a tree
Strong for a column, spear-straight for a pillar?"

They know of only one possible tree, the one "guarded by garlands of silver." Solomon has it felled; but try as they will, the carpenter cannot fit it into its socket in the Temple. So Solomon has it laid within the Temple, "as our chief and dearest treasure."

Placed in the temple with it are its thirty circles of silver, which are the thirty pieces of silver later paid to Judas. After the hallowing of the temple, the tree remains fixed, even when five hundred men try together to move it.

But when Maximilla prophesies that "the God of heaven" will be crucified on it by the Jews, the holy beam is repudiated. And now it is found that it can be moved, and the priests have it carried away and cast into the Pool of Bethesda. Its presence causes an angel to come and stir the water, so that "the halt are healed and the sick made whole." So then the priests have it cast into the brook of Kedron, where it serves as a bridge.

By this bridge the Queen of Sheba prepares to cross, on her visit to King Solomon; she too, recognises the holy beam, prophesies its future, and humbly fords the brook on foot. By the time of Christ the beam has a reputation of being accursed, which is why the Executioners choose

to make Christ's Cross from it, because:
"If the beam is accursed, why, so is Christ,
And cross and felon shall well agree."
After the Crucifixion, the Cross burst into blossom.
Joseph of Arimathea begged for the Cross as well as for
the Body; but by then the Cross had been buried in a
secret place, where it remained hidden till the Empress
Helena was led to it by her vision. The lily-crucifixes to
be found in only twelve English churches and the
burgeoning cross of Glastonbury refer to the end of this
legend, which Dr. Steiner makes transparent when he
tell us:
"Christ unites himself with the Cross; the higher nature
is drawn into the lower, and then the wood of the cross
becomes a *living* power."
We see then that Percivale's sister is touching on deeply
esoteric matters when she speaks of the six spindles to
the three knights. We can understand, too, with what
power holy Imaginations rooted in this legend were
working in the soul and sheaths of Malory's medieval
readers when they entered the Ship of Solomon with his
three Grail heroes.

Percivale's sister now relates to her three knight-
neophytes how a Voice informed King Solomon that the
last of his lineage should be a man who was a pure
maid. Taking counsel with his wife, with her aid he
built this ship, and had the rich bed made, and bade a
carpenter cut the spindles from the white, the green and
the blood-red tree.
It was at her advice that Solomon had King David's
sword brought forth from the temple and put into the

ship; and for this sword she herself made its present poor girdle of hemp, directing that it was to be replaced by a worthier one made by the hands of a virgin princess when the right time came.

And now that time *has* come. Here, on the Ship of Solomon, is the last of Solomon's lineage, the knight who was a pure maid. Percivale's sister takes from a coffer "girdles that were seemly wrought of golden threads and upon which were set full precious stones and a rich buckle of gold."

"Lo, Lords," says she, "Here is a girdle that ought to be set about the sword. The greatest part is made of my hair, which I loved well while I was a woman of the world. But as soon as I wist that this adventure was ordained me, I clipped off my hair, and made this girdle in the name of God."

And she sets the girdle of her golden sun-wisdom on the girdle made by Solomon's wife.

She gives to the sword a name, "The Sword of the Strange Girdles." She gives to its sheath the name, "Mover of Blood" – "for no man that hath blood in him ne shall never see the one part of the sheath that was made of the Tree of Life."

For the sheath is made of snakeskin. It has therefore a certain transparency. And since a snake's casting of its skin is connected with a rhythm of renewal, the sheath made of snakeskin has also a connection with renewal, but here where physical are lifted to spiritual levels. The sheath is the physical body; while man's blood still runs red with passion instead of having the innocent transparency of the flower's sap, the transparent archetypal body of man as he was before the Fall and as he will be again in the far distant future is hidden from him. For man's original physical body was the first spindle as white as snow; and it will be again as white as snow when it has been transmuted into Spirit-Man.

In Grail and Arthurian literature a reference to the sheath of the sword frequently carries an esoteric undertone. Thus, Merlin once asked King Arthur which he counted the more precious, Excalibur or its sheath.

"Excalibur," replied Arthur.

"You are wrong," Merlin told him. "It is the sheath that is the more precious."

And when Morgan le Fay steals Excalibur's sheath by water, she turns herself to stone as soon as she steps ashore. For she would use for impure magical purposes the forces of what, at the end of human evolution, will be a copy of Christ's own Resurrection Body.

Galahad now begins to grip the sword, explaining to Bors and Percivale that it is "for to give you courage; for wit ye well that it belongeth no more to me than it doth to you." With these words the conviction is first borne in upon us that Wolfram's Parzival and Malory's Galahad are souls of different epochs. For it is central to Parzival's situation that he should be a solitary seeker after the Grail. But from the beginning is it made clear in *Le Morte d'Arthur* that, whatever variations there may be in actual achievement of the Quest, Galahad draws to him a Grail fellowship.

Now Percivale's sister girds him with the sword.

"Now I hold me one of the most blessed maidens in the world," she says, "who hath made thee now the worthiest knight in the world."

"Damosel," replies Galahad, "ye have done so much that I shall be your knight all the days of my life."

This is far more than a graceful expression of courtesy. It expresses an exact esoteric relationship, the relationship between initiator and initiated. For the bond of destiny forged between two beings by such a shared spiritual experience is an occult reality.

"Then they went from that ship, and went into the other." The initiation is over. "The wind drove them apace" back to the material world.

They landed in the marshes of Scotland; and, having delivered the Earl Hernox from prison, all four were present at mass in a chapel on a waste forest to which a white hart and four lions had led them.

"And at the secrets of that mass, they saw the hart become a man, and set him upon the altar in a rich siege; and they saw the four lions changed, the one to the form of a man, and the other to the form of a lion, and the third into an eagle, and the fourth unto an ox."

The Sun-stag of pagan Christianity – the Christianity of the Arthur stream –gives place to the Christ-Jesus of the Evangelists, as he was esoterically understood in the Christianity of the Grail stream. Galahad, Bors and Percivale are still knights of the Round Table, but to this they have now united the knighthood of the Grail.

Immediately following this mystical experience, the four approach a castle from which there issues forth a gentlewoman bearing a silver dish, accompanied by a train of armed knights.

Percivale's sister is asked:

"Are you a maid?"

When she affirms that she is, the train of armed knights demand:

"This gentlewoman must yield us the custom of the castle. What maid that passeth hereby shall give this dish full of blood of her right arm."

"Blame have ye,"cried Galahad, "that brought up such customs!"

And he, with his sword of the strange girdles, and with "his two fellows helping him passing well," fought with three score knights, "doing such marvels that all who saw him weened he had been none earthly man."

At nightfall a truce was called, and Percivale's sister and her three knights were offered harbourage in the castle. There they enquired concerning its evil custom.

They were told that the lady of the castle was sick of a leprosy, and the only help for it was a dish full of the blood of a virgin who was a King's daughter, "and for this thing was the custom made."

Then said Percivale's sister:

"There shall be no more battle. Tomorrow I shall yield you the custom of the castle."

On the morrow, when they had heard mass, Percivale's sister bade them bring her to the sick lady, and they let her blood till the dish was filled.

She lifted her hand and blessed the lady, saying:

"Madam, I am come to my death to make you whole."

Then she swooned away.

The three knights raised her and staunched her blood. When she came out of her swoon, she said:

"Fair brother Percivale, I must die for the healing of this lady. As soon as I am dead, put me in a boat and let me go as adventure will lead me. As soon as ye three come to the city of Sarras, to achieve the Holy Grail, you will find me there before you. Bury me there in that spiritual place."

As soon as she had received the bread and wine, her soul went forth. And that same day the lady was healed of her leprosy.

" Then Sir Percevale made a letter, of all that she had holpen them, as in strange adventures, and put it in her right hand, and so laid her in a barge, and covered it with silk; and so the wind arose, and drove the barge from the land, and all the knights beheld it till it was out of their sight.

"Then all drew all unto the castle; and so forthwith there fell a sudden tempest of thunder, lightning and rain, as all the earth would have broken. So half the castle turned upside down; so it passed evensong or the tempest was ceased.'

And when, after many adventures, Christ sent the three knights to Sarras in that same Initiation-Ship of Solomon, they found Percevale's sister there before them, "and buried her as richly as a King's daughter ought to be."

In *Le Morte d'Arthur*, Percivale's sister has no name. In his poem,*The Last Voyage*, Charles Williams calls her Blanchefleur, perhaps as an echo of Gautier's description of Dindrane – "*blanc com fleurs en may novele.*" He forges for her an immortal Epitaph:

"She died another's death; another lived her life."

This is a line of noble poetry which is at the same time an occult truth. In making a gift of her purified blood, she made a gift of her life. Compassion flowers in her into immediate deed. Her death becomes a microcosmic human echo of Christ's on Golgotha.

One is reminded of Albert Steffen's play, *Alexander's Transformation*, in which the sick girl gives up her purified body to the murderess, Roxane. Rudolf Steiner has indicated this offering up of one's own substance as a future method of exercising love.

"Whoever is really able to pour forth love on his fellow-creatures can quicken, comfort and elevate them by his love alone.

"Evolution consists in the acquisition of an increasing capacity for sacrifice, until a being is finally capable of offering up his own substance and being; indeed, of feeling it to be his highest bliss when he gives forth what he has developed as his substance.

"Such sublime beings do indeed exist, who rise to a higher level of existence by offering up their own substance."

In this way the hierarchy we know as the Thrones poured out their substance to create the first incarnation – the Saturn incarnation – of our Earth. When we reach Vulcan, the Earth's final incarnation, humanity will have reached that stage of sacrificial creation.

Rudolf Steiner was so sparing of definitions (he preferred characterisations) that the few he did give carry the more weight. One of these few sums up the whole course of human evolution through all the seven incarnatuions of the Earth – Saturn, Sun, Moon, Earth, Jupiter, Venus, Vulcan: "Man is a being who rises from receiving to giving."

If, then, in Lohot, we can see a certain picturing forth of man in relation to his own mortality on distant Jupiter, in Percevale's sister perhaps we already also glimpse in miniature the love-capacity of mankind on still more distant Vulcan.

REFERENCES

Ordinalia 14th Century. Translated from the Cornish.
The Last Voyage, Charles Williams. *In Taliesin Through Logres.*

LECTURES by RUDOLF STEINER:

Concerning the Temple Lost and Rediscovered,
   See in "The Temple Legend"
   Berlin, 15 May-5 June 1905.

The Gospel of St. John and its Relation to the Other Gospels, (Cassel) 24 June-7 July 1909.
   (Anthroposophic Press).

CHAPTER VI

THE WANDERING VIATICUM

In Wolfram's epic, *Parzival*, as also in the opera, *Parsifal*, which Wagner founded on it, the home of the Grail is Montsalvat. Here it stays, always, secluded – indeed, protected– by sixty leagues of pathless forest. When a Grail knight is to go forth to serve the outer world, the message appears on the Grail in letters of gold. But the Grail itself never leaves the Grail Castle.

In Malory's *Morte d'Arthur* there is also a kind of Grail Castle – Carbonek, the home of King Pellease and his daughter Elaine. Here both Lancelot and Bors twice separately experience the presence of the Grail; and at its last appearance, on the occasion of its withdrawal from thence to Sarras,"that spiritual city," so do the "three white bulls," Galahad, Percivale and Bors. But Percivale and Ector are also healed by it in the forest; Launcelot sees it heal a sick knight in a ruined chapel; and it appears in terrible splendour to the assembled Round Table at Camelot.

The Grail also "goeth about" in Gautier's Continuation of Chrétien de Troyes *Conte del Graal*,where an angel bears it into the forest to heal the wounds of Parsifal and Hector, and where on another occasion Parsifal and a damsel see a great light when the Rich Fisherman carries it through the forest by night for protection.

Thus in England the Grail wanders from place to place. On this level, therefore, it fulfils the descriptive title given to Rudolf Steiner for it by the Norwegian Folk-Spirit – "*ganganda greida*," The Wandering Viaticum.

In the *Valthrudismal*, Odin refers to himself by the name *Gangradr*, the Wanderer. His wanderings are not in the earth-realms but in the world of etheric forces, in Goethe's Realm of the Mothers. It is to this realm that the Grail belongs.

In Malory the Grail Quest itself also takes a different form from that in Wolfram. In Wolfram only Parzival may find the Grail; and only those whose names appear upon it may serve it. They serve it – like Parzival – withdrawn within the Grail Castle, or – like Lohengrin – sent out to rule some kingless country or to plant some new impulse into human evolution.

But in Malory all the hundred and fifty knights of King Arthur's Court go in quest of the Grail, though, except at Whitsuntide at Camelot, when its presence is experienced by the entire Round Table, it appears to only five of them, apart from the sick knight who is not named. Naciens the hermit explains why to Gawaine:

"The cause is that is appeareth not to sinners. For ye be an untrue knight and a great murderer."

"Sir," said Gawaine, "It seemeth me by your words that for our sins it will not avail us to travel in this quest."

"Truly," said the good man , "There be hundred such as ye be that shall never prevail."

In Malory the Grail makes nine appearances to Knights of the Round Table – Launcelot experiences its presence five times, Bors four times, Percevale and Galahad three, Ector once and all the assembled knights of King Arthur's Court once, when it feeds them at Camelot.

But during his childhood in his grandfather's castle of Carbonek, first in Elaine's arms, and later at King Pelleas' knee, before he was taken to the White Nuns to be educated, Galahad had lived always in its holy atmosphere. One can even surmise that his first coming to Camelot and the Grail's appearance there on that same Whit Sunday were spiritual events invisibly related.

In the unfolding of the story of the first of these appearances, we have picture placed beside picture in a closely-woven and most significant pattern.

First, one Whit Sunday, a hermit comes to King Arthur's Court, and as the knights sit at meat he asks them why one seat –the Siege Perilous – at the Round Table is void.

They tell him:

"There shall never none sit in that siege but one, but if he be destroyed."

And *he* in turn tells *them*:

"This same year he that shall sit in the Siege Perilous shall be gotten, and he shall win the Sancgreal."

When the feast is over, Sir Launcelot rides out in search of adventure. He comes to a tower, wherein lies a lady in great pain, "for she boileth in scalding water until the best knight of the world shall take her by the hand. By enchantment Queen Morgan le Fay and the Queen Northgalis had put her there in that pains, by cause she was called the fairest lady of that country."

Launcelot takes her by the hand, and the enchantment is broken.

Full of joy, they enter a chapel to give thanks; and here the people tell them how they go in fear of a serpent living in a nearby tomb. Launcelot fights and slays the serpent; and on the tomb he finds written in letters of gold:

"Here shall come a leopard of King's blood, and he shall slay this serpent, and this leopard shall engender a lion, the which shall pass all other knights."

And this is indeed a true prediction. For though in all else Launcelot is the best knight in the world, his feeling-life is sullied by his liaison with Queen Guenever – he is a leopard, a lion of impure blood. But the feeling-life of the son who is to be born of him will be pure – he will be a lion passing all other knights."

King Pelleas, the king of that country (it is known as the Foreign Country), escorts Launcelot to his castle. It is the Castle of Carbonek, in Britain the home of the Grail.

"And anon there came in a dove at a window, and in her bill there seemed a little censer of gold, and therewith there was such a savour as though all the spicery of the world had been there. And forthwith there was upon the table all manner of meats and drinks that they could think upon.

"So there came a damsel passing fair and young, and she bore a vessel of gold between her hand, and thereto the King kneeled devoutly, and said his prayers, and so did all that were there.

"'Oh Jesu,' said Sir Launcelot, 'what may this mean?'

"'This is,' said King Pelleas, 'the richest thing that any man hath living. And when this thing goeth about, the Round Table shall be broken. And wit ye well that this is the Holy Sancgreal ye have here seen.'"

"And when this thing goeth about, the Round Table shall be broken." Already we have the first intimation of that approaching disintegration of the increasingly worldly Arthurian Knighthood which will be brought about by the appearance of the Grail at Camelot.

When we contemplate the Grail's approaches to Launcelot, we become aware of the spiritual world's patience and perseverance with a prodigal son of royal stature. Again and again he is given the opportunity fully to achieve this Quest. Again and again he is hindered by what is still untransmuted in him. Again and again, outspoken hermits do not fail to tell him so plainly.

Nevertheless, the first appearance of the Grail, other than to its guardians at Carbonek, is to this noblest of the Arthurian knights, marred only by this one flaw; for it is pre-ordained that he shall be the father of the purest Grail-knight, and that this very night this son shall be conceived.

King Pelleas knows that the chosen mother is his own daughter Elaine, and has schooled her in her duty. But he wonders much how this thing shall come about, seeing that Launcelot is so besotted on Queen Guenever.

Then Dame Brisen, "one of the greatest enchantresses that was at that time in the world living," brought Launcelot a cup of wine, "so that he weened that the Lady Elaine had been Queen Guenever. With ye well that Sir Launcelot was glad, and so was the Lady Elaine, for well she knew that the same night Sir Galahad should be begotten, that should prove the best knight in the world."

Next morning Launcelot rose and went to the window." And as he unshut the window, the enchantment was gone." At first he was highly incensed, "for there was never a knight so deceived as I am this night," but Elaine tells him gently that "I have obeyed me unto the prophecy that my father told me, and have given the

fairest flower that ever I had; and therefore, gentle
knight, owe me your goodwill." At which Launcelot
"took his leave mildly of her."

As soon as the child was born, "they named him
Galahad, for because Sir Launcelot was so named at the
font stone.' We can thus see Launcelot's baptismal
name as pointing to his higher self. The lower self
(Launcelot) cannot itself fully achieve the Grail-quest;
but it can give birth to a higher self (Galahad) which
can.

In Dame Brisen's enchanted wine we can see the forces
of destiny working.

As in pre-Christian times the Essenes had arranged
marriages with the future mission of the race in mind,
so King Pelleas and Dame Brisen act as hierophants at
the coming together of the chosen parents of the knight
who is the chosen of the Grail.

Thus, in this, the Grail's first appearance in Malory, we
can perhaps think of it as hovering over the pure soul
descending from the stars; as drawing this rare being
down to his earthly habitation as later he was to draw
the Grail to those about him; as overshadowing his
entry into incarnation.

If we think of Launcelot as representing the Arthur
stream, and of King Pelleas as representing the Grail
stream in so far as it yet existed in Britain (which would
explain his kingdom being known as the Foreign Country), we can perhaps see in the conception of Galahad
the first preparation for a prophetic mingling of these
two streams in this one rare being five hundred years
before that historic mingling, of which Dr. Steiner tells
us, took place.

When Bors, Launcelot's nephew, find the way to Carbonek, he is young and untried, and we are expressly
told that "for all women he was a virgin, save for one
only that was the daughter of King Brandegoris." King
Pelleas tells him that Gawaine had lately been at the
castle, "but found little worship there." To Gawaine the
Grail had not revealed its presence.

"And ever Sir Bors beheld the child Dame Elaine had
in her arms, and ever him seemed it was passing like Sir
Launcelot." When Elaine tells him, "Wit ye well that
the child is his," he weeps for joy.

Here, for the first time, one a stripling knight, one a
babe in arms, meet two of the "three white bulls" who
are to go together through the solemn Initiation of the
Ship of Solomon, and who, at Christ's bidding, are to
carry the Grail out of Logris. And upon this momentous
meeting the Grail straightway bestows its blessing; the
child whose conception followed the Grail's first
appearance to an Arthurian knight is present in his
mother's arms at this, its second appearance.

"There came in a white dove, and she bare a little
censer of gold in her bill; and anon there was all manner of meats and drinks; there was a maiden that
bare the Sancgreal. They kneeled down and made their
devotions; and there was such a savour as all the spicery in the world had been there. And when the dove
took her flight, the maiden vanished away with the
Sancgreal, as she had come."

Bors sits bemused.

"What ye mean in this castle I wot not," he said. "But
ye have many strange adventures. Therefore I will lie in
this castle this night."

King Pelleas counsels against this; but Bors persists,
and, having been shriven, is left alone in "a fair, large

chamber." And here he meets adventures reminiscent of
Gawain's in Wolfram's Chastel Merveil.

First a spear launches itself at him, large and long; its
head, burning like a taper, wounds him in the shoulder.
Bors is so nearly immaculate that we can perhaps see in
this spear "the sorrow of all who know that they suffer
from the forces that kill their nobler selves." It is like a
far-off echo of Amfortas' wound.

Next he fought with a knight, and overcame him. Then
came flights of arrows; then a lion, "but with his sword
Sir Bors smote off his head." Lastly, he witnessed a battle between a dragon and a leopard.

"Then an old man entered the hall, and he sat down in
a fair chair, and there seemed to be two great adders
about his neck. And then the old man had a harp, and he
sang an old song, how Joseph of Aramathy came into
this land."

And then he tells Sir Bors:

"Full worshipfully have ye done; and better shall ye do
hereafter."

And now Bors experiences the presence of the Grail
again, but this time in far greater measure. The first
slender glimpses of the Grail expand; its Sanctuary and
its attendants now also become visible. For the first
time we hear of the Grail's table of silver, which we are
to see again and again in its later appearances. Silver
belongs to the etheric; in this context we can perhaps
think of the table of silver as a clairvoyant vision of the
etheric body.

"Then Sir Bors seemed that there came the whitest
dove that ever he saw, with a little golden censer in her

mouth; and anon therewithal the tempest ceased and passeth, that before was marvellous to hear. So was all the court full of good savours.

"Then Sir Bors saw four fair children that bare four tapers, and an old man in the midst of the children, with a censer in his one hand, and a spear in his other.

"And then Sir Bors saw four gentlewomen enter into a chamber where was great light, as it were a summer light. They kneeled before an altar of silver, with four pillars. And he saw as it had been a bishop kneeling before that table of silver.

And as Sir Bors looked up, he saw a sword like silver, naked, hovering over his head; and the clearness thereof smote so in his eyes that, at that time, he was blind,

"And he heard a voice that said:

"'Go thee hence, thou Sir Bors; for as yet thou art not worthy to be in this place.'

"Then he went backward to his bed. And on the morrow King Pelleas made great joy of him.

"And then he departed, and rode to Camelot."

To Camelot Bors brought tidings that "Sir Launcelot had gotten a child by fair Elaine, whereof Queen Guenever was wrath and gave Sir Launcelot many rebukes." King Arthur, returning from his wars in France, "Let cry a great feast, and all lords and ladies should be there." Among the ladies was Elaine.

Though Queen Guenever lodged her in a chamber near her own, Elaine's heart was heavy, for Launcelot would not look at her. But by enchantment Dame Brisen again brought Launcelot and Elaine together. In the night

Queen Guenever heard Launcelot "Clattering as a jay"
in his sleep of his love for herself." Then was she nigh
out of her mind and coughed so loud that Sir Launcelot
awaked; then he knew that he was not with the Queen.
"He leapt out of bed, and the Queen met him in the floor,
crying:
"'Be not so hardy, though false traitor knight, as ever
again to come into my sight.'"
Launcelot leapt from the window, "and ran forth he
knew not whither, and was mad as ever was man. And
so he ran two years, and never man might have grace to
know him."
Many knights of the Round Table went out separately in
many directions in search of him; and among these were
Sir Ector and Sir Percivale. Percivale was the third of
the "three white bulls" whose destiny was to be so intimately interwoven with the Grail's withdrawal into
higher worlds. Ector was Launcelot younger brother.
Wolfram's Parzival, when he first sets out on his Grail-
Quest, is so naive that, having slain his first knight, he
doesn't know how to strip him of his armour. In the same
way, Malory's young Percivale does not yet know his
own strength.
In one encounter during the search for Launcelot which
leads him to his first experience of the Grail, "within
awhile he had slain all that would withstand him; for he
dealt so his strokes, that were so rude, that there durst
no man abide him.'
In the adventure that followed, in which he freed a
knight chained to a marble pillar, "he drew out his sword
and stroke at the chain with such a might that he cut it in
two, and went on through the knight's hawberk, and
even hurt him a little."

And in the third adventure, which was to bring the Grail to his help, he met a knight in single combat, "and they fought near half-a-day, and never rested them but little; and neither had less wounds than fifteen; and both bled so much that it was marvel that they stood upon their feet. For this knight that fought with Sir Percivale was a proved knight, and a well-fighting; and Sir Percivale was young and strong, but not knowing in fighting as the other was."

At last Percivale begs the other to tell him his name, "for I was never or this time matched. "The other, confessing that "never no manner of knight has hurt me so dangerously as thou hast done." tells him that he is Sir Ector de Maris, brother of Sir Launcelot du Lake. Percivale wails that he is Sir Percivale de Galis, "that have made my quest to seek Sir Launcelot and now I shall never finish it, for ye have slain me." But Ector insists that it is he who is slain;" but tell not my brother Launcelot ye have slain me or he will be your mortal enemy; but say that I was slain in my Quest as I sought him."

Percivale "kneeled down and made his prayers devoutly, for he as one of the best knights of the world that was at that time, in whom the very faith stood most in.

"'Right so there came by the holy vessel of the Sancgreal, with all manners of sweetness and savour. Sir Percivale had a glimmering of that vessel and of the maiden than bare it. And forthwith they were both as whole of limb and hide as ever they were in their life days, wherefore they gave thanks unto Almighty God, right devoutly."

Said Percivale:

"What may this mean, that we be thus healed, and

right now we were at a point of dying?"
Said Ector:
"I wot well what it is. It is an holy vessel that is borne
by a maiden, and therein is a part of the holy blood of
Lord Jesu Christ."
Said Percivale again:
"So God me help, I saw a damsel all in white, with a
vessel in both her hands, and forthwithal I was whole."
Then they mended their harness and mounted their
horses and continued their quest for Launcelot together.
This,the fourth appearance of the Grail, is the first in
which it "goeth about the world."

Meanwhile, while knights of the Round Table sought
high and low for him. Launcelot "ever ran from place to
place, and lived by fruit and water for two years; and
other clothing had he little save his shirt and his
breeches." The erring soul must wander, suffer and lose
itself, before by the healing forces of the Grail it is made
whole.
He falls foul of a savage wild boar – "this boar hath
bitten me right sore," he tells the hermit who nurses
him. We are reminded that it was those companions of
Odysseus who were a sensual nature who under
Circe's enchantment turned into swine.
His bodily wounds healed, but not his mind, Launcelot
ran from the hermitage through a forest, and so came to
the City of Corbin, and ran through it into the castle of
Carbonek, with all the youths of the city pursuing him.
And here the squires rescued him from his tormentors,

"and ordained clothes unto his body, and straw underneath him, and a little house, and every day they would throw him meat and set him drink."

At the feast of Candlemas, King Pelleas knighted his nephew, Castor, "who gave many gowns; and he sent for the fool, that was Sir Launcelot, and gave him a robe of scarlet, so the he was the seemliest man in all the court, and none so well made." He strayed into the garden and went to sleep beside its well; and here one of Elaine's maidens found him. And when she brought Elaine to look at him, Elaine, loving him, knew him.

She reports her discovery to King Pelleas, who has Launcelot carried "into a tower, and so into the chamber where was the holy vessel of Sancgreal. By that holy vessel he was laid, and there came a holy man and opened the vessel. And so, by miracle and by virtue of the holy vessel, Sir Launcelot was all healed and recovered."

This account of the healing of Launcelot's madness by the Grail is given by Malory with the greatest reticence and reserve. One is conscious that here are intimations of a sacred mystery that is kept veiled.

King Pelleas gives to Launcelot and Elaine "a castle on an island, enclosed with iron, with a fair water, deep and large. Sir Launcelot let call it the Joyous Isle, and there he was called none otherwise but le Chevalier mal Fet, the knight that hath trespassed." And here they lived, secluded, till Percivale and Ector, still searching together for him, found him there.

Ector prevails upon Launcelot to return with them to
Court, to be present at the great feast of Pentecost. At
their departure, Elaine reminds Launcelot:
"My Lord, at this same feast of Pentecost shall your son
and mine, Galahad, be made knight, for he is full fifteen
years old."
At Camelot, "the King and all the knights made joy of
Sir Launcelot. And the Queen wept as she would have
died, and then afterwards made great joy."
At the vigil of Pentecost a gentlewoman came to
Camelot, and begged Launcelot to come with her,
promising the Queen that he should be with the Court
again in time for tomorrow's high feast.
"They rode till they came into a forest, where he saw an
abbey of nuns; and they led him into the abbess's
chamber and unarmed him. And already there before
him was his nephew, Sir Bors.
Twelve nuns came in to them, bringing Galahad. They
said:
"Sir, we bring here this child, the which we have
nourished. And we pray you for to make him a knight."
"Sir Launcelot beheld that young squire, and saw he
was seemly and demure as a dove; he weened of his age
never to have seen so fair a man of form."
He asked:
"Cometh this desire of himself"
And all, including Galahad, answered:
"Yea."
So on the morrow, at the hour of prime, Launcelot
made his son a knight, saying:
"God maketh him a good man, for beauty faileth him not
as any that liveth."
So Bors for a second time is present at a high moment
of Galahad's destiny.

That day when all the knights came back from the Pentecost service at Camelot minster, each found his name written in letters of gold over his seat at the Round Table. But over the Siege Perilous was written:
"Four hundred winters, and four and fifty, accomplished after the passion of our Lord, ought this siege to be fulfilled."
And,reckoning, Sir Launcelot said:
"It seemeth me this siege ought to be fulfilled this same day."
So they covered the letters with a silken cloth, "till he come that ought to achieve this adventure."
A squire comes in to report a marvel – a stone floating in the river, and from the stone a sword protruding. The whole Court goes out to see it. On the pommel of the sword, written in "subtle letters of gold," they read:
"Never shall man take me hence, but only he by whom I ought to hang, and he shall be the best knight of the world."
King Arthur calls on Sir Launcelot to "essay it;" but he refuses. Then he calls on Sir Gawaine; but "he might not stir it." Next he calls on Sir Percivale, who "drew at it strongly, but he might not once move it. Then were there no more that durst be so hardy to set their hands thereto."
Sir Kaye, the Seneschal, with all the responsibilities of the great feast awaiting them on his mind, now pointedly reminds the King:
"Now may ye go unto your dinner, for a marvellous adventure have ye seen.'
"So all went back, and every knight knew his own place, and set them therein; so they were served, and all the sieges fulfilled, save on the Perilous Siege.
"Then all the doors and windows of the palace shut by

themselves; and an old man in white came in, and with him a young knight in red arms, without sword or shield, save a scabbard hanging by his side."

The young knight saluted them:

"Peace be with you, fair lords."

The old man said to him:

"Sir, follow after."

He led him to the Siege Perilous,"where next beside sat Sir Launcelot," and lifted the silken cloth. And now the letters it had hidden read:

"This is the siege of Sir Galahad,the noble prince."

The old man told the young knight:

"Sir, wit ye well this place is yours.

Then Sir Galahad "set him down surely in that siege, and all the knights marvelled greatly that he durst, and he so tender of age; for there sat never none but he was mischieved.

"Then Sir Launcelot held his son, and had great joy of him, and Sir Bors told him follows:

"Upon pain of my life this young knight shall come unto great worship."

Then King Arthur, having welcomed him, took Sir Galahad by the hand, and went down with him to the river, to show him the sword in the stone.

He said to Sir Galahad:

"Here is great marvel as ever I saw; and right good knights have assayed and failed:

But Sir Galahad made answer:

"Sir, that is no marvel. For this adventure is not theirs but mine. And for surety of this sword I brought none with me; for here by my side hangeth the scabbard."

And he lightly drew the sword out of the stone, and slipped it into his scabbard, saying:

"Now it goeth better than it did aforehand."

As they returned to the palace they were met by a damsel, who thus greeted King Arthur:

"King Nasciens the hermit sendeth thee word that to thee shall befall the greatest worship that ever befell king in Britain. For this day the Sancgreal will appear in this thy house, and feed thee and all the fellowship of the Round Table."

And so it was.

For when they had all been to Evensong in the great minster, and had returned to the palace for supper, and were seated each in his own place, "anon they heard cracking and crying of thunder, that them thought the place should all to drive. In the midst of this blast entered a sunbeam more clearer by seven times then ever they saw, and all they were alighted of the grace of the Holy Ghost.

"Then began every knight to behold other; and either saw other, by their seeming, fairer than ever they saw before. Not for then there was no knight might speak one word for a great while; and so they looked every man on other as though they had been dumb.

"Then there entered into the hall the Holy Grail covered with white samite; but there was none might see it, nor bare it. And there was all the hall fulfilled with good odours, and every knight had such meats and drinks as he best loved in this world.

"And when the Holy Grail had been borne through the hall, then the holy vessel departed suddenly, that they wist not where it became. Then had they all breath to speak. And the King yielded thankings to God, of His good grace that He had sent them. 'Certes,' said the King, 'we ought to thank our Lord Jesus greatly for that he hath showed us this day, at the reverence of his high feast of Pentecost.'"

Now this was the Grail's sixth appearance.

Yet for Gawaine this did not suffice.
He cried:
"We might not see the Holy Grail. It was preciously
covered. Therefore tomorrow I shall labour in quest of
the Sancgreal for a twelvemonth and a day."
Sad though this made King Arthur, the rest of the fellowship of the Round Table were fired to do likewise.
Some of the ladies would also have gone with their lov-
ers; but Nasciens the hermit sent word that "he that is
not clean of sin shall not see the mysteries of our Lord
Jesus Christ."
Next day a hundred and fifty knights gathered for a last
service in the minster. Then "they mounted upon their
horses, and rode through the streets of Camelot, and
there was weeping of the rich and poor, and the King
might not speak for weeping."
So the Quest of the Grail began.
Each knight followed his own path and met with his
own adventures. Sir Launcelot, riding headlong through
a wild forest, came one night to a stone cross, with an
old chapel, "broken and wasted," nearby.
Within the ruins he saw light from six great candles in a
silver candlestick set on a fair altar. But when he tried
to enter, he could find no way in. So he pastured his
horse and lay down to sleep on his shield near the old
stone cross.
Half-waking, half-sleeping, he saw two white palfreys
approaching, bearing a sick knight on a litter. The
lighted candlestick moved without hands towards the
stone cross. Before this there now stood a table of silver,

and on it the holy vessel of the Sancgreal.

The sick knight prayed:

"Fair sweet Lord, that is here within this holy vessel, make me whole of my great malady."

Then he drew near to the table on his hands and knees, and kissed the holy vessel. And then he cried again:

"Lord God, I thank Thee, for I am healed!"

After a great while, the holy vessel went back into the chapel, with the candlestick and the light; and the healed knight rose to his feet, and kissed the cross, and presently departed.

But Launcelot lay there in a stupor.

Then he heard a voice that said:

"Sir Launcelot, more hard than is the stone, more bare than is the fig-tree, go thou from hence; withdraw thee from this holy place."

And Launcelot cried:

"When I sought worldly adventures, ever I achieved them. But now that I take upon me the adventure of holy things, mine old sin hindereth me, so that I had no power to stir nor speak when the holy blood appeared afore me."

This is a cry from the heart. Launcelot is only too painfully aware of what has happened – that a second time the Grail has approached him and proffered itself to him, and he, out of an inner inhibition, has been unable to respond. Malory specifically stated that Launcelot has been "half sleeping and half waking" (that state known to the alchemists as a portal to illumination), and that the Grail had waited for his response "a great while" before withdrawing, but that he was "so over-taken with sin that he had no power to rise ageyne (towards) the holy vessel."

His horse and his harness had vanished, annexed by the

sick knight who had been healed, so Launcelot went on
foot through the forest till he came to a mountain, and
on the mountain a hermitage where a hermit was about
to say mass.

When this was over, they talked together, and Launcelot told him what the voice by the stone cross had
said. The hermit replied:

"Sir Launcelot, man shall not find one knight to whom
our Lord has given so much grace as He hath given to
you. But thou wilt not leave thy sin for no goodness that
God hath sent thee. Therefore are thou more hard then
any stone; and never wouldst thou be made soft nor by
water nor by fire; and that is why the hete of the Holy
Ghost may not enter into thee. Moreover, where over-
much sin dwelleth, there may be but little sweetness;
and therefore art thou likened also to the barren fig-
tree.When the Holy Grail was brought before thee,
there was found in thee no fruit."

And when the hermit had furnished him with a horse
and harness, Sir Launcelot, chastened, departed.

After much wandering, Sir Launcelot "came to the
water of Morteise, and lay down and slept. In his sleep
a voice bade him enter into the first ship he should find.
"And when he had heard these words, he started up,
and saw a great clearness about him. He came to a
strand, and found a ship without sail or oars; and as
soon as he was within the ship, he felt the most sweetest
savour that ever he felt, so that he cried:

"Fair Father, Jesus Christ, I know not in what joy I am,
for this joy passeth all earthly joys that ever I was in."

On a fair bed he found the body of Sir Percivale's sister,

with a writing in her hand setting forth the story of her death. For a month or more he was with her; and "every day, when he said his prayers, he was sustained with the grace of the Holy Ghost."

One night he heard the galloping of a horse. It stopped on the strand, and a young knight entered the ship. So met father and son; "for," said Sir Galahad, "you were the beginning of me in this world." They dwelt together within the ship for half-a-year, "and served God daily and nightly with all their power."

Then, one day, they sailed to the edge of a forest, and there a knight awaited them, armed all in white and leading a white horse. He bade Sir Galahad leap upon the horse and ride in quest of the Sancgreal. So father and son parted; and a wind arose "and drove Sir Launcelot more than a month throughout the sea, where he slept but little and prayed unto God that he might have a sight of the Holy Sancgreal."

And at midnight the ship sailed towards the postern of a castle, "and the moon shined clear." A voice said:

"Launcelot, go out of this ship, and enter into the castle, where thou shalt see a great part of thy desire."

He entered the castle, between two lions, and came to a closed door behind which a voice sang sweetly. He kneeled before the door and prayed:

"Fair sweet Father, Jesu Christ, show me something of that I seek."

The door opened, "and there came out a great clearness, so that the house was as bright as though all the torches of the world had been there. And in the midst of the chamber he saw a table of silver, and the holy vessel covered with red samite, and many angels about it. And before the vessel he saw a good man, clothed like a priest."

As the good man lifted the vessel on high,it seemed to Launcelot as if he would have fallen, and he entered the chamber to help him. A breath of fire smote him to the ground; he lost consciousness and was borne out by many hands; and for four and twenty days and nights he lay in a swoon,"which he thought was a penance for the four and twenty years that he had been a sinner.'

We are reminded of how he was chidden by the hermit after his stupor at the wayside cross, "for your presumption to take upon you in deadly sin for to be in His presence, where His flesh and His blood was; for He will not appear where such sinners be, but if it be unto them great hurt and their great shame."

His importunate prayers have been granted. He has been permitted to look upon the Grail again, this time even in its own sanctuary. But it has been a desecration of the sanctuary to bring into it unsanctified desires to which, in self-will, his soul-nature still clings, in spite of the hair shirt he now wears upon his body.

When Launcelot recovered, King Pelleas (for the castle was Carbonek) made much of him, revealed who he was, and broke to him the news that the Princess Elaine, King Pelleas' daughter and the mother of Sir Galahad, was dead.

"Right so as they sat at their dinner in the chief hall, all the doors and windows of the place were shut without man's hand. Then was it so that the Sancgreal fulfilled the table with all manner of meats that any heart may think.

But it remained invisible, and Launcelot was told:

"The Quest of the Sancgreal is achieved right now in you. Never shall ye see more of the Sancgreal than ye have seen."

So sadly he returned to Camelot.

And now events on every level and in every realm began to move towards each other in preparation for the last and most solemn appearance of the Grail in Britain.

First, Galahad and Percivale, riding out of a great forest, came to a "travers", and there met Bors riding alone. "It is no need," comments Malory, "to tell if they minded."

The three rode on together to Carbonek, where King Pelleas received them with joy. His son, Eliazer, brought to them a broken sword with which Joseph of Arimathea had been wounded in the thigh. Bors tried to mend it, and failed. Percivale tried to mend it, and failed. But as soon as Galahad drew the pieces together, the sword was as if newly forged. By common consent it was given to Bors.

As evening drew on,"the sword rose up, great and marvellous, and was full of great heat. And a voice lit among them, that said:

"They that ought not to sit at the table of Jesu Christ, arise."

Then those who ought not withdrew, leaving only Galahad, Percivale, Bors, King Pelleas, his son and his niece. To them, entered nine knights, three from Gaul, three from Ireland, three from Denmark, saying:

"Sir, we have hied sore to be with you at this table, where the holy meal shall be parted."

Then four gentlewomen brought in a bed, in which lay a sick king wearing a golden crown, who said:

"Galahad, knight, ye be welcome. Long have I desired your coming."

And a voice cried:

"There be two among you who be not in the quest of the Sancgreal. Therefore depart ye."

Whereupon King Pelleas and his son rose and departed. Then it seemed to those who remained that four angels came from heaven, bearing in a fair chair a man in bishop's vestments, and with letters on his brow which read:

"See ye here Joseph, the first bishop of Christendom."

They set him down before a table of silver, whereon the Sancgreal stood, and other angels bore in candles, a towel, and a bleeding spear. Then Joseph consecrated the bread and wine; "and at the lifting up of the wafer, there came a figure in the likeness of a child, and the visage was as bright as any fire, and smote himself into that bread."

And when all was done that should be done, Joseph kissed Galahad, "and bade him kiss his fellows; and as he was bidden, so he did."

Then said Joseph:

"Now before this table shall you be fed with sweetmeats such as never knights tasted."

"Then looked they and saw a man come out of the holy vessel, that had all the signs of the passion of Jesus Christ, bleeding all openly, and said:

"My knights and my servants and my true children, receive now the high meat ye have so much desired.'

"Then took he himself the holy vessel, and came to Sir Galahad, who kneeled down and there received his Saviour; and after him received all his fellows; and it seemed to them of a sweetness that was marvel to tell."

Then said he to Galahad:

"Thou must go hence, and likewise this holy vessel; for now it shall depart from the realm of Logris. Take no

more with you than Sir Percivale and Sir Bors. Go you
three tomorrow unto the sea, where ye shall find your
ship ready."

Then, having blessed them, he vanished from their
sight.

Then Galahad went to the bleeding spear, and touched
it, then touched the sick king upon the bed. And at once
he was made whole. And at midnight a voice told the
rest of the company to depart; and they did so.

Galahad, Percivale and Bors rode for three days, till
they reached the strand where their ship* awaited
them. When they came on board, they found the table
of silver already there, and on it the Sancgreal, covered
with red samite. They entered, and "made great reverence thereto." Then they set sail.

And in such wise was the Holy Grail taken out of Britain.

---

*The Ship of Solomon.

LECTURES by RUDOLF STEINER:

Christ and the Spiritual World,
  Leipzig, 28 Dec,1913-2 Jan.1914.

Karmic Relationships, Vol. 8. (R. Steiner Press).
  Torquay, 12-21 Aug. 1924.

GENEALOGY OF HERODIAS AND SALOME

HEROD THE GREAT
married

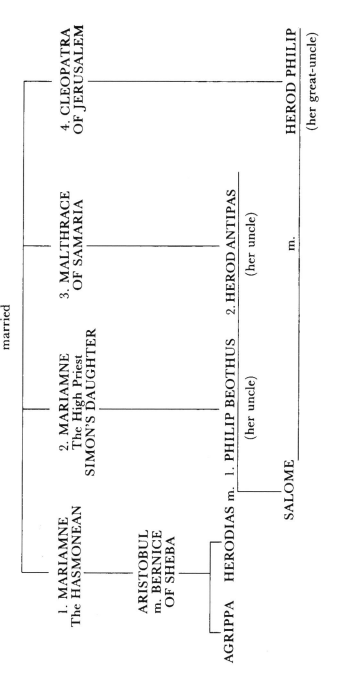

1. MARIAMNE
The HASMONEAN

2. MARIAMNE
The High Priest
SIMON'S DAUGHTER

3. MALTHRACE
OF SAMARIA

4. CLEOPATRA
OF JERUSALEM

ARISTOBUL
m. BERNICE
OF SHEBA

AGRIPPA   HERODIAS m.   1. PHILIP BEOTHUS   2. HEROD ANTIPAS

(her uncle)   (her uncle)

SALOME   m.

HEROD PHILIP

(her great-uncle)

CHAPTER VII

KUNDRY-HERODIAS
Herodias

K undry," says Rudolf Steiner, discussing Wagner's *Parsifal*, "has already lived once as Herodias, who asked for the head of John the baptist, Herodias, the mother of Ahasver." We therefore ask ourselves; How far can her earlier incarnation as Herodias throw light on her later Grail incarnation as Kundry?

Herodias was the grand-daughter of Herod the Great, the Herod of the Massacre of the Innocents. From the Gospel of St. Matthew we already know the turbulence of the blood she inherited from him.

Her grandmother, Mariamne (the first of Herod's eight wives) was a Hasmonean princess – that is, she belonged to the great Jewish house of the Maccabees, so that all their drive and will-power also ran in the veins of Herodias, to be used either for good or for evil.

Through her mother, Berenice of Sheba, Herodias inherited the Star-wisdom of Arabia, which again could be dedicated to the white path or the black and be powerful in either.

When Herodias was two years old, her father was strangled at her grandfather's orders, and her mother fled to Rome with her sons, leaving her daughters behind. At the age of five Herodias was betrothed by

Herod to her Uncle, Philip Boethus, his son by his second wife. In due course the marriage took place, and Salome was born of this marriage within close blood ties.

By a third wife, Malthrace of Samaria, Herod had a further son, Herod Antipas, who was Tetrarch of Galilee and Peraea. Of him Josephus tells us:

"This Herod of Tetrarch was married to the daughter of the King of Petra. But on his journey to Rome (he was a close friend of the Emperor Tiberius) he lodged with his stepbrother, Philip Boethus, with those wife he fell in love. He arranged with her to come to him on his return from Rome, when he would divorce his wife. This settled, he sailed to Rome."

On his return to Galilee, Herodias forsook one uncle to marry another, taking Salome with her. Herod Antipas at this time was fifty years old, and Herodias thirty-seven.

What followed is recounted thus in St. Mark's Gospel:

"This same Herod had sent and arrested John and put him in prison at the instance of his brother Philip's wife, whom he had married. John had told Herod: 'You have no right to your brother's wife.'

"Thus Herodias nursed a grudge against him, and would willingly have killed him, but she could not, for Herod went in awe of John, knowing him to be a good and holy man; so he kept him in custody. He liked to listen to him, although listening left him much perplexed.

"Herodias found her opportunity when Herod on his birthday gave a banquet to his chief officials and commanders and the leading men in Galilee. Her daughter came in and danced, and so delighted Herod and his guests that the king said to the girl:

'Ask what you like and I will give it to you.'
And he swore an oath to her:
'Whatever you ask I will give you, up to half my kingdom.'
She went out and said to her mother:
'What shall I ask for?'
She replied:
'The head of John the Baptist.'
The girl hastened back at once to the king with her request:
'I want you to give me here and now, on a dish, the head of John the baptist.'
"The king was greatly distressed, but out of regard for his oath and for his guests he could not bring himself to refuse her.
"So the king sent a soldier of the guard with orders to bring John's head. The soldier went off and beheaded him in the prison, brought the head on a dish, and gave it to the girl, and she gave it her mother.
"When John's disciples heard the news, they came and took his body away and laid it in a tomb."
This image of a bleeding head in a dish was a profaning of the Mysteries of the Holy Grail." What was at work there," says Steiner, "was nothing less than black magic."
Herodias, then, stands before us as a black magician, working out of the forces of those ancient close blood-relationships which by then had become evil, because though legitimate in the time of the Pharoahs, the time of their legitimacy was now past. We see them pictured in her marriage to her two uncles, and again in her giving Salome in marriage to the brother of both her own husbands.
The head belongs to the past; and the impure blood-

forces whose time is outworn are elevated in this anti-
Grail Mystery. But for Herodias there is even something more; it is a particular head that is sacrificed –
the head of John the Baptist, the preparer of the way for
the Christ whose pure blood is to be the true content of
the Grail.

But Herodias has not in actual fact achieved what she
had intended – she has not destroyed the further working of the Grail's preparer.
John the Baptist has passed through an inner beheading
– he has sacrificed his past, his towering pre-Christian
stature, in order to become the herald of the Christ. The
beheading by Herod makes outwardly manifest this
inner and spiritual change. Herodias, by bringing about
this beheading, has actually freed the already Christ-
ened being of John to work supersensibly in and
through the Twelve surrounding Jesus of Nazareth.
The might of this overshadowing is reflected immediately in the increase of power which made possible the
feeding of the five thousand. And a distorted wisp of the
truth was even dimly apprehended by the people, for a
rumour was spread abroad that John had risen from the
dead.
Something of the character of Herod Antipas is revealed
in his reaction to this.
We have already heard that he "liked to listen" to John.
Now St.Luke tells us:
"Herod said:
"'As for John, I beheaded him myself; but who is this I
have heard such talk about?'
"And he was anxious to see him."

He is curious about the miracles wrought by Christ-
Jesus, Who sends this message to him by the Pharisees:
"Go tell that fox: today and tomorrow I shall be casting
out devils and working cures; on the third day I reach
my goal."
And later,when Pilate sends Jesus to Herod:
"When Herod saw Jesus he was greatly pleased; having
heard about him, he had long been wanting to see him,
and had been hoping to see some miracles performed by
him. He questioned him at some length without getting
any reply. Then Herod and his troops treated him with
contempt and ridicule, and sent him back to Pilate
dressed in a gorgeous robe."
Christ does not answer Herod's idle curiosity, though
He does answer Pilate's honestly perplexed questions.
"That fox" is a picture of the sharp intellect. Herod
shows, not heart-warm interest, but cold intellectual
curiosity; and in the end he mocks what he does not
understand.
But behind him, directing his actions, work the
Luciferic heat and abandonment of Herodias. There is
even a legend that she was present at the mocking of
Christ; that it was she who caused Him to be gorge-
ously arrayed in a parody of the Mysteries; that she
laughed at Him in derision, and that for this she is
doomed to await His Second Coming.

Like an outward projection of this working together of
their disparate natures is the duel landscape in which
Herod Antipas and his wife Herodias move.
Herod Antipas is Tetrarch of Galilee and Peraea. The
landscape of Galilee is fresh, beautiful, brimmed with

those etheric forces which, as Dr.Steiner has said, can
be either chaste or unchaste. But at its heart was
Tiberias, with its hot springs, its glow and fever, its
Roman worldliness and licence. It is Herodias, one
feels, who holds the reins of Galilee and who binds its
exuberant etheric forces to serve her own dark ends.

Peraea, by contrast, is a desert on the sinister borders of
the sub-earthly Dead Sea. Like the Antipas-intellect, it
is petrified and dried-out. And four thousand feet above
the bitter waters of the Dead Sea, with only the iron
chasms and crags of the Mountains of Moab between,
stood the gaunt fortress of Machaerus, in which John
was imprisoned and beheaded.

This is an Antipas-landscape. Yet even here Herodias
imposes her will on Herod's, as the unbridled desire-
nature is able to do with the dried-out intellect. It is
significant that it was at the beginning of spring that
John's beheading took place; in connection with the
feeding of the five thousand which immediately followed
it, St. John's Gospel says, "Now the Passover was at
hand." So all those upsurging creative forces which on
Good Friday revealed to Wagner the Mystery of the
Grail were harnessed by Herodias to a deed of black
magic.

"Through white magic," Dr. Steiner tells us, "the Earth
will ever more and more approach the nature of the
Sun; through black magic the nature of the Moon. If
the forces of black magic got the upper hand, it would
lead to the hardening of the earth-sphere, so that it
became a moon. The forces which, in sun and moon,
have been separated out, were developed out of the

substances of the earth; they are always present in the strata of the earth.

"The forces developed by a black magician lead to the increase of those forces which belong to the demonic nature of the earth."

The task of the second half of earth-evolution is the etherising of the earth into a new sun. We see Herodias, therefore, as an opponent of this task; it is into moon that she would turn the earth.

We see, too, the spiritual truth behind the legend which makes her the mother of Ahasver. While St. John awaits Christ's Second Coming because his own time is not ripe till then. Ahasver also must wait it because he has rejected Christ's first coming and all the powers of progress it bestowed. In Ahasver that has hardened and petrified which in his race should, at Christ's coming have dissolved and passed away.

In due course, the Roman Emperor Tiberius, the royal friend and patron of Herod Antipas, was succeeded by Caligula, who for boon companion had had for many years Herodias' brother, Agrippa.

Till now the Herods had ruled the various provinces of Palestine only as Ethnarchs or Tetrarchs under a Roman governor. But now, 38 A.D., Caligula sent his friend Agrippa to Trachonitis, not as Tetrarch (an office which Salome's husband Philip had held there), but as King. Nothing would satisfy Herodias but that Herod Antipas and she herself should similarly become *King* and *Queen* of Galilee; and she gave Antipas no rest until he agreed to journey with her to Naples to extract these titles from Caligula.

But there a very different reception awaited them from the one Herodias has triumphantly envisaged. For her brother Agrippa had written to warn Caligula, quite untruthfully, that Herod Antipas was plotting against him. Caligula's welcome, therefore, was to strip them of all titles, offices and possessions, and to banish them as outcasts to Gaul.

One of the Emperor's entourage reminded Caligula that Herodias was his friend Agrippa's sister, Caligula thereupon offered in her case to revoke the sentence of banishment.

Herodias replied with dignity:

"You, O Emperor, offer pardon in a magnificent manner, as becomes you. But the love which I have for my husband prevents me from accepting your favour. For it is not right that I, who have been his partner in prosperity, should forsake him in his misfortune."

So, together, stripped of all they valued in life, Herod Antipas and Herodias passed out of the presence of the Emperor, to live out the rest of their lives mutely and ingloriously in Gaul.

Five years earlier, on the cross of the repentant thief on Golgotha, the great rebellious spirit, Lucifer, had been in prototype redeemed. This was known to the Early Church Fathers. St. Gregory of Nyassa, for example, says:

"Through the Crucifixion, good was done, not only for all lost creatures, but also for the Author of our perdition.'

But the corona of Luciferic spirits have their own freewill. Dr.Steiner tells us that they had till the year

869 A.D. to be redeemed – the year in which the Arthur
Christianity met the Grail Christianity, the year in which
the cosmic Christ met the Christ in the hearts of men.
Steiner speaks of Christ and Lucifer as in a certain
respect changing places, in that Christ becomes inner
and Lucifer outer. Those unredeemed Luciferic impulses which still work in *man*, should, if and when
redeemed, be working from the periphery of universal
thinking, bringing enlightened thought. (We glimpse
here something of the mystery of the connection of
Lucifer with the Holy Spirit). If one may think of that
meeting of the two streams as the moment of Christ
becoming inward, we can see why the year 869 A.D. is
the point at which the Luciferic spirits have finally to
decide whether to follow the way of evolution – i.e. by
becoming outward, or whether to continue working,
now wrongfully, *within* man.

In the light of all this one can see the deed of Herodias
in accepting poverty and banishment with her husband
in dignified freewill as the first seed of redemption of
the Luciferic impulses that worked so powerfully in her,
for here was the first lifting of sensual into selfless love.
Dr. Vreede's* astronomical researches indicate the year
of 828 A.D. as that of Parzival's achievement of the
Kingship of the Grail. In the reincarnation of Herodias
as Kundry in the ninth century, therefore, we may look
with hopeful heart-warmth for further stages of redemption of the Luciferic being working in her before the
year 869 marks the close of their respite.

We have two records of that Kundry-incarnation, one

---

*Dr. E.Vreede was leader of the Mathematical-Astronomical
Sec-tion of the School of Spiritual Science at the Geotheanum,
Dornach, Switzerland, from 1924-1935.

in Wolfram von Eschenbach's epic, *Parzival*, one in
Richard Wagner's opera, *Parsifal*. They are astonishingly different, yet wholly reconcilable.

Wolfram's Kundry

In Wolfram, though Kundry is spoken of as a sorceress,
she plies no sorcery, but rides freely to and fro across
the closely guarded frontiers of the Grail-territory as the
Messenger of the Grail – the accredited messenger, her
raiment woven all over with the turtle-doves of the
Order.
Not only does she, mounted on her mule, bear tidings
from Montsalvat, hidden in sixty leagues of trackless
forest, to its knights in the outer world, but she also
gives practical care to the solitaries who devote their
lives to God in seclusion in the wilds. Thus, when Parzival meets his cousin Sigune for the second time, she is
now living as an anchoress. Through her small window
she tells him how she survives:
"There comes to me some provision sent hither from
the Grail. The Sorceress Kundry takes thought for that;
each Saturday, without fail, she brings me food for the
whole week following."
Kundry's first appearance on the stage of Parzival's life
is a stormy and forbidding one.
King Arthur's Court is gathered at an outdoor feast,
seated in a flowery meadow, about a great circle of silk
laid on the grass to represent the Round Table. To this
feast Parzival, fresh from his victorious combats with
the Arthurian knights, is brought by Gawain.

He is received with great rejoicing."He undid his helmet, and through the iron-grime his skin shone fair…
Young Parzival, standing there, lacking naught but wings, seemed an angel this earth had budded … When women saw him, their looks spoke welcome through their eyes into their hearts he came … God was in a pleasant mood when he created Parzival:
Everyone loves him at first sight; and King Arthur is prepared to make him a Knight of the Round Table. But in this epic that would be the wrong destiny for Parzival. Already, though his own awkwardness has so far obscured this, he has been marked out to be the future Grail-King. He is saved from taking the wrong step by Kundry, who comes riding her mule furiously across the plain.
Kundry is monstrous and misshapen. Her eyes are yellow, her lips purple. She has hair like hogs' bristles, a nose like a dog's, ears like a bear's, skin like a monkey's, claws like a lion's, tusks a hand's breadth long. She wields a knotted scourge.
She is the counterpart of all that this angel without wings still bears unconsciously within him.
She denounces Parzival as a traitor, as a false and faithless guest who has neglected to heal his suffering uncle, Amfortas, of his wound by asking the compassionate question,"Sir, what ails you?'
She cried:
"You look on me with horror, yet far comelier than you am I. Sir Parzival, speak if you can, and tell me why, when the sad Fisherman sat by you, lorn of hope and lorn of joy, you brought no release from sorrow? Ah, Montsalvat, home of sorrow, alas that there is none to comfort you!"
Already a first hint of his tragic error has been cast at

Parzival when the Grail squire had reviled him as he
left the castle, calling after him:
"Goose that you are! Could you not have opened your
beak and put to your host a question?"
His cousin Sigune, too, whom he had found weeping in
the forest, her slain husband, Schionatulander, across
her knees, had lamented on hearing that he had not
asked the question, calling him dishonoured and
accursed.
And now with this third repudiation, this repudiation
by Kundry, he has the shattering experience of standing
fallen and stripped before this company of the flower of
chivalry, confronted, in Kundry's loathliness, with the
untransmuted being within himself.

So Parzival sets out again on his wanderings, he, says
Wolfram, "whom Kundry with harsh words drove forth
to seek the Grail."
But nowhere can he find the way back to Montsalvat.
After many adventures, he again finds his cousin
Sigune, now living as an anchoress. She tells him:
"The sorceress Kundry rode past just now. Ride after
her. Perchance she is not yet so far but that you may
with good speed outride her."
He obeyed, and "came at once on that fresh track. He
followed; but so wild became the way which Kundry's
mule had followed that the forest maze soon blotted out
all trace of guidance.
"And thus once more the Grail was lost to him."
For Parzival is still riding a horse with short ears – that
is, his own thinking is still bound to and by sense-
impressions. He has to acquire a Grail-horse – he has to

break through to a higher state of consciousness –
before he can rediscover the Grail Castle.

He fights and defeats a Grail knight, and takes his
horse, with the Grail turtle-dove on its trappings." He
let the reins fall on the horse's neck; and the steed led
him straight to a place he knew, Montsalvat Fountain,
where lived Trevrizent the Pure."

And here his hermit uncle unfolds to him the meaning
of the Good Friday Mystery, and gently leads him
further along his inner path.

This time he makes no sudden leaps, but reins quietly
and modestly." If God has hate towards me, I will bear
it." He meets, and fights with, and makes friends with,
his pagan brother, Fierifis, "he who was striped black
and white like the pages of a book." And Fierifis he
takes to King Arthur, who welcomes him with joy.

Once again King Arthur's Court is seated in a flowery
meadow, grouped about a silken Round Table on the
banks of the River Plimizoel. It is like a kind of
archetypal repetition of that earlier occasion.

For the striving of the Round Table was after a world-
embraciveness which Parzival had lacked on the first
occasion; otherwise he would not have failed to put the
healing question. But now he has it. His being is
enlarged to embrace his pagan brother. Now it would
be in his nature to put the healing question.

So now a second time Kundry comes pricking her mule
across the plain. And now she is no longer loathly.

She cries to Parzival:

"Be glad, yet humble withal! The inscription on the
Grail is read; you shall be lord thereof.

"Condwiramur your wife and your son Lohengrin to
share that honour are elected, also.

"Yes, and were all this lacking, one thing granted you

would prove you blessed –that now a question from your mouth shall free King Amfortas from pain."
Parzival asks humbly and courteously:
"Lady, when shall I set out for my home of joy?"
And Kundry tells him:
"In the name of the help you bring, make no delay."
Kundry also tells him that he may take one companion with him, and for that companion he chooses his brother Fierifis. So, with Kundry as guide, the two brothers set out for Montsalvat.
"As they come near an outpost, its captain, seeing the emblem of the turtle-dove shine, multiplied, from Kundry's raiment, said to his band: "Our cares are ended. Stay still! For unto us great joy is coming."
"So all dismounted and, standing on the grass with bare heads, received Sir Parzival. His greeting rang in their ears like words of blessing.
"More people than could be numbered received them with warm welcome at the foot of the palace stair. Rich garments were brought them to wear, and wine was poured for them. Then Amfortas, that sorrowful man, received them, saying:
"'I have waited wearily for you. Blest shall you be if it lies in your power to help.'
"Then Parzival, weeping, fell thrice on his knees, in honour of the Trinity, and prayed that that sorrowful man might be freed from pain. Then he rose to his feet and said:
"'Uncle, what ails thee?"
"And He Who bade Lazarus arise, gave back health and strength to Amfortas. Colour and warmth returned to him; his skin glowed radiant as a flower in bloom. There was never a man so beautiful as Amfortas when his sickness left him. God's skill is wonderful."

So it was Kundry, she who in her loathliness had with
harsh words driven him forth to seek the Grail, who
now brought Parzival to its Kingship, he who now "was
of all men's beauty the flower, nay, more than that, the
flower-wrought crown." It was Kundry who, rehearsing
the Arabic names of the planets on their inward sweep
from Saturn to Moon, revealed to him the far-flung
domain of that Kingship:
"All that the circle of these stars encompasses, lies
within your reach, to be attained and won."

Wagner's Kundry

The grim and tragic presence of Herodias stands close
behind Wagner's Kundry. We may marvel at the con-
tinuity of evil in human karma until we reflect that
while, after death, "a man has been receiving moral
impulses in kamaloca to correct his wrong-doing, his
Double in the interior of the earth has at the same time
been receiving the reflection of these impulses."
Kundry's black magic practices as Herodias have brought
her now under the domination of the master of black
magic, Klingsor, so that the two impulses battling within
her cause her to lead a double life. When she is fully
awake and mistress of herself, she is humble and contrite,
a servant of the Grail, longing only to be used in the service of good.When Klingsor exercises his mastery over her
in hypnotic sleep, she is bewitched and bewitching, and is

used as a tool by him in the service of evil.

She has a swarthy complexion, and her black eyes are "now flashing, now fixed and glassy." her laughter is wild and frenetic, as if an echo of that of Herodias at the mocking of Christ. She is still a heathen.

"Kundry can only achieve complete purification," says Dr.Steiner, "in that noblest and purest form of Christianity which manifests in Parsifal. She has to remain a black enchantress until Parsifal releases her."

The note of magic and of duality is struck early in the opera by Kundry's arrival with balsam from Arabia for Amfortas' wound, which she herself has been instrumental in causing. She has been to fetch the balsam on her enchanted mare, which can travel as easily in the air as upon the earth. Gawain has also brought a remedy; but Gurnemanz, Amfortas' armourer, sighs knowing that the only remedy is the arrival of Parsifal, the Pure Fool:

"Fools are we to hope thus for his healing
When only one thing healeth."

He recalls the part Kundry had played in the wounding of Amafortas:

"Close under the fortress, the young king was separated from us.
A woman of appalling beauty had bewitched him.
In her arms he lay entranced
The lance dropped from his hand;
A cry of unearthly agony resounded.
Klingsor vanished, laughing, bearing away the sacred spear."

Gurnemanz recounts to the young squires how, when Titurel, Amfortas' grandfather, built the Grail Castle, none but the pure in heart might enter, and therefore Klingsor was refused admittance.

"Powerless to kill sin in his soul, he laid a guilty hand upon his body, and this hand he again stretched forth against the Grail. Its guardian spurned him. At this he was enraged, and fury disclosed to him that his infamous act could give him counsel in the use of wicked magic. He transformed the desert into a garden of delight wherein flourish women of devilish beauty, and thither he lures the Grail-Knights to sinful joys. Those he entraps become his slaves."

Klingsor, meanwhile, from a window in a tower in his Castle of Perdition, is watching the approach of Parsifal, the Pure Fool.

"My magic castle lures the fool!" he rejoices.

Now from Kundry's body, which he has put into a deep trance, he conjures forth her astral being in a violet mist. As she comes forth she shrieks in terror, and begs to be allowed to die rather than be forced to continue tasks of such a devilish nature.

Nevertheless, on Parsifal's arrival, Kundry, subservient now to Klingsor, and now enticingly beautiful, calls him by name, and amid the rampant blossoms that seek to smother him, breaks the news of how his mother, Herzeleide, has died of sorrow at his leaving her. Parsifal is overcome with contrition. But when Kundry takes him in her arms consolingly and kisses him on the lips, he starts away from her in horror.

"Amfortas! The wound! The Wound! It burns in my heart!"

Laying aside the wiles of fascination, Kundry now appeals to his compassion.

"Do you feel in your heart others' sorrow?

Feel then also mine!
Through endless ages I have awaited the Saviour
Whom once I dared to mock.
Did you but know the curse
Which tortures me unendingly!
Let me be united with you for but one hour,
And in you I shall be redeemed."
But Parsifal firmly replies:
"Rather would you be damned with me for evermore
If I forgot my mission
For your salvation also I am sent,
Will you but refrain from desire."
Cursing Parsifal's path, Kundry cries aloud on Klingsor
to wound him also with the lance. Appearing on the
battlements above the garden, Klingsor casts the lance
at Parsifal, but it hovers poised over the Pure Fool's
head, as the demon lance does above Buddha's in his
temptation by Mara.
Parsifal grasps it out of the air and with it makes the
sign of the cross, with the solemn words:
"With this sign I exorcise your magic!"
The castle crashes. The garden turns back again into a
desert. With a wailing of despair, Kundry staggers and
falls amid the ruins.

Parsifal, lance in hand, sets out again on his long search
for the Grail Castle, to bring healing to Amfortas.
It is on Good Friday that he comes again to Gurnemanz, and with him finds Kundry, clad now in the
rough garment of a penitent. She washes his feet,
annoints them with precious ointment from a golden
phial, and dries them with her hair.

From the spring beside them Parsifal takes water in the
hollow of his hand. With it he sprinkles Kundry's head,
with the blessed words:
"Be baptised!"
For the first time, Kundry weeps. It was a mark of
medieval witches that they could not weep. Kundry is
no longer a sorceress.

The Grail is unveiled. Before it Parsifal heals Amfortas'
wound by touching it with the lance which had caused
it, and with the words:
"Be whole, purified and redeemed!
Blessed by thy suffering,
Which gave pity and pure knowledge to the timid
Fool!"
When the healing lance has been restored to the sanctuary, Parsifal elevates the Grail. A beam of clear light
descends to it, and in the light a white dove.
Kundry, redeemed, accepted, falls dead at Parsifal's
feet. The desire she, as Klingsor's slave, had represented has been transmuted. Her Herodias-karma has
been worked out.

In Wolfram, on Parzival's first visit to the Grail Castle,
the Grail procession has been preceded by a bleeding
lance which a page carried through the hall. At the
sight of it, says Wolfram, "there was weeping and wailing throughout the wide palace; the people of thirty
lands could not have wrung so great a flood from their
eyes."

When Parzifal comes to Montsalvat a second time, "after the very sure assurance Trevrizent had seen written on the Grail" that this time he would ask the healing question, the bleeding lance is no longer there. Wolfram does not explain this; but Wagner makes it clear that it is only when it is misused that the sacred love-lance of the sun becomes the bloody lance.

Rudolf Steiner speaks of this lance as the ray from the sun which calls forth the power which lies in the blossom, chaste in the plant world, but in man and animal mingles with desire and passion. With the holy lance, as with the Holy Grail, its white magic (Chrétien de Troyes actually describes the lance as *white*) can be turned into its opposite in blasphemous hands.

We see in Wagner's Parsifal how this happened in the case of Klingsor. Under that name, Rudolf Steiner tells us, were grouped together remnants still left, in the Middle Ages, of old degenerate Mysteries. He speaks also of the Klingsor-danger in extreme asceticism – "Klingsor has mutilated himself so as not to fall a prey of the senses, but has not overcome his desires." (In fact, as Gurnemanz points out, his self-mutilation has added power to his black magic). And with that impulse inimical to the Grail of which the Lord of the Moors and Aristot of Moraine in *Perceval li Gallois* make us conscious, Klingsor also has his connections. The actual personality who was his historical prototype, Count Landulf II of Padua, who lived in Sicily in the ninth century, had deep Arabian entanglements.

In Wagner, Parsifal is not immune to Kundry's temptation. But he transmutes that temptation into a fellow-feeling for Amfortas, whereupon the lance refrains from wounding him but hovers above his head, so that he is able to retrieve it, to exorcise Klingsor's black magic with it, and with it eventually to heal Amfortas' wound. Can we perhaps see here a prophetic picture of the path by which the Grail Castle will become what its name indicates –Montsalvat, the Mount of healing?

REFERENCES

Josephus, *Antiquities of the Jews.*
Gospel of St. Mark, VI, 17-29 New English Bible.
Gospel of St. Luke, IX, 9 New English Bible.
Gospel of St. Luke, XII, 32 New English Bible.
Gospel of St. Luke, XXIII, 8 New English Bible.
Valentin Tomberg, *Studies in the Old Testament.*

LECTURES by RUDOLF STEINER:

Richard Wagner in the Light of Anthroposophy,
 Berlin, 28 March and 19 May 1905. See NSL 175-8.

White and Black Magic Contrasted,
 Berlin, 21 Oct. 1907. Typed Z 306.

Parsifal,
 Berlin, 19 May 1905 (4th lect. of R. Wagner above),
 Landin/Mark, 29 July 1906. "The Christian Mystery"
 (Completion Press).

KING ALFRED'S GRAIL GENEALOGY

CHARIBERT VON LAON

BERTA married PIPPIN II

CHARLEMAGNE

CHARLES THE BALD (grandson)

JUDITH

ALFRED THE GREAT

GENEALOGY OF THE TOWN-FOUNDERS

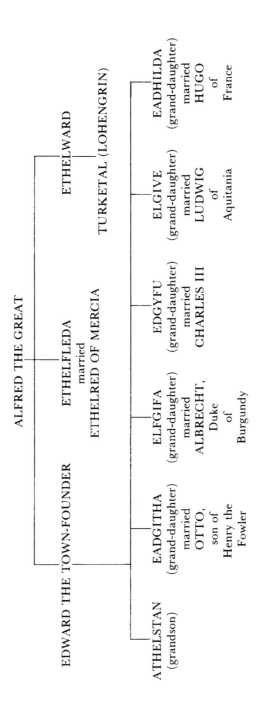

ALFRED THE GREAT

EDWARD THE TOWN-FOUNDER

ETHELFLEDA
married
ETHELRED OF MERCIA

ETHELWARD

TURKETAL (LOHENGRIN)

ATHELSTAN
(grandson)

EADGITHA
(grand-daughter)
married
OTTO,
son of
Henry the
Fowler

ELFGIFA
(grand-daughter)
married
ALBRECHT,
Duke
of
Burgundy

EDGYFU
(grand-daughter)
married
CHARLES III

ELGIVE
(grand-daughter)
married
LUDWIG
of
Aquitania

EADHILDA
(grand-daughter)
married
HUGO
of
France

CHAPTER VIII

THE TOWN-FOUNDERS

Rudolf Steiner tells us that the Arthur stream and the Grail stream met in 869 A.D. and presently united. From its earliest beginnings in distant pre-Christian times, the Arthur stream, centred in Great Britain, had striven to bring civilising impulses not only to this island but also into Northern, Central and Western Europe.

The Grail Stream, coming from the East and spreading from Spain, established on Montsalvat its spiritual castle from which Grail initiates came forth to bring new impulses into European evolution.

Following the meeting in 869, therefore, one would expect, looking below the surface both of Continental and of English history, to find each fertilising the other, and to find them working together in bringing to birth such new impulses.

And so, indeed, we do.

Flor and Blanchefleur, an alchemical legend first written down by Conrad Fleck in 1220, tells how King Phenix of Spain gives a captive lady to the Queen, his wife, and how the Queen bears a son and the captive lady a a daughter at the same hour on the same day in the same palace. Because the day is Palm Sunday (*Paskie florie*), the little prince is given the name Flor, and the little captive girl the name Blanchefleur.

The children were devoted to each other. Conrad tells us:

"The two loved each other already
When they were not yet five years old."

When this childhood love continued into adolescence King Phenix, troubled, sent Prince Flor to be educated in Andalusia, promising that in due course Blanchefleur should join him there.When time went on and she did not come, Flor returned to his father's court to fetch her, and was told that she was dead.

He was shown a magnificent tomb on which they were both depicted:

"Thereon Flor sweetly, tenderly,
Offered his love a rose
Skillfully shaped in red gold,
While graciously she held out to him
A lily fashioned in burnished gold."

In his grief Flor would have killed himself. To prevent this he was told the truth, which was that the Queen his mother had sold Blanchefleur to merchants from Babylon.

Flor set out at once in search of her, riding a horse red on one side and white on the other. It led him to the tower of the Admiral of the East in a land ruled by seven kings. In the tower's seventy rooms dwelt seventy ladies, who waited on the Admiral, two by two. Here Blanchefleur, whom the Admiral had bought from the Babylon merchants, waited on him in her turn with Claris, her friend.

By playing chess with the guardian of the tower, Flor wins his confidence, and when the guardian's servants carry a basket of flowers up to Claris's room, Flor, muffled in a red mantle and covered with red roses, is concealed in it, and he and Blanchefleur meet again with joy,

For some days Flor remains hidden in Blanchefleur's room, till one morning when she should have been on duty she oversleeps. In the late thirteenth century English version of the legend, the scene which follows is told with great humour. The steward who is sent to fetch Blanchefleur returns to say she is asleep in the arms of Claris and that they look so beautiful that he cannot bear to disturb them. The Admiral turns and points behind him; there stands Claris with her embroidered towel, awaiting Blanchefleur's arrival with the silver bowl of water for the Admiral's toilet!

The Admiral has Flor and Blanchefleur taken to his Judgement Hall, and sentences them both to death. Flor begs that only he should be slain, since Blanchefleur is innocent. Blanchefleur begs that only she should be slain, since it was on her account he came. The Admiral rules that they must both be slain; he unsheathes his sword and bids them both kneel down before the block. But each held back the other and strove to be beheaded first.

The Judgement Hall was filled with the sound of the onlookers' weeping at this "loving strife and counter-strife." They cried out with one voice that never had they found two so true and selflessly of one mind. They begged the Admiral to have mercy on this innocent pair, till at last his heart melted and his sword fell from his hand.

So Flor and Blanchefleur were wedded, and returned in

joy to Spain, where Flor rules the kingdom well and nobly after King Phenix's death, till they were a hundred years old. When they in turn died, they died as they had been born – at the same hour on the same day in the same place. They were buried in the same grave, out of which there sprang a rose and a lily, intertwined. Conrad gives them this moving epitaph:
"Never could false love enter
Where these two came."

Songs concerning the Red Knight and the Lily were very dear to the hearts of the twelfth century Low German minstrels. Muffled in his red cloak, covered with red roses, Flor is seen as such a knight.

On the tomb we see the two children holding out to each other rose and lily. The ancient wisdom saw the lily as a picture of pristine purity; its bulb is a paradise-plant; it still looks heavenward; it loves water; it is not fully at home upon the earth.

But the rose roots strongly into the soil on earth; it holds a balance between above and below. Flor is the son of King Phenix; as in the Phoenix Mysteries, his forces go through death and resurrection; the sense-nature is not negated, but lifted to the pure sap of the rose.

Already the Rose Cross Meditation hovers above this story; already the coming light of Rosicrucianism shines prophetically into it.

Conrad tells us:

> "To this loving pair
> A Child, a lovely maid,
> Had been given, named Berta.
> Form this Berta and from Pippin
> Was Charlemagne born."

Berta, Pippin, Charlemagne – these are historical figures, whose dates and lineage are known to us. Pippin
and Berta were married in the year 741; Charlemagne
was born to them in 742.
Who then was Flor?
Berta's father "in real life" was Charibert von Laon.
What part did he play in evolution that such a legend
should be woven about him?

In 769 A.D., exactly a hundred years before the Arthur
stream and the Grail stream met, Charibert von Laon
instituted the Fellowship of the Holy Grail.
Anthroposophy tells us:
"On a small scale it is the same in the spiritual worlds
as when we sow a grain of corn in the earth; it germi-
nates, and blade and ear spring from it, bearing innum-
erable grains which are replicas of the *one* grain of corn
we had laid into the earth. In this multiplication of the
grain of corn we can perceive an image.
"When the Mystery of Golgotha was accomplished,
through the power of the indwelling Christ the etheric
body and astral body of Jesus of Nazareth were *multiplied*; ever since that time, many replicas have been
present in the spiritual world.
"Such an etheric body was woven into great bearers of

Christianity on the 4th, 5th, 6th, to 10th centuries – for example, Augustine.

"Such an astral body was woven in the 11th to the 14th centuries to Francis of Assisi, Elizabeth of Thüringen, etc.

"Replicas of the 'I' of Jesus of Nazareth, multiplied many times, are present now in the spiritual worlds.

"The outer, physical expression of the 'I' is the blood. There have been men whose task it was, through the centuries since the Event of Golgotha, to ensure in secret that humanity gradually matures, so that there may be human beings who are fit to receive the replicas of the 'I' of Christ-Jesus of Nazareth.

"To this end it was necessary to discover the secret of how, in the quietude of a profound mystery, the 'I' might be preserved until the appropriate moment in the evolution of the Earth and of humanity. With this aim a Brotherhood of Initiates who preserved the secret was founded: the *Brotherhood of the Holy Grail*.

"This fellowship has always existed. It is said that its originator took the chalice used by Christ-Jesus at the Last Supper, and in it caught the blood flowing from the wounds of the Redeemer on the Cross. He gathered the blood, the expression of the 'I', in this chalice – the Holy Grail.

"And the chalice of the blood of the Redeemer, with the secret of the replica of the 'I' of Christ-Jesus, was preserved in a holy place, in the brotherhood of those who, through their attainments and the Initiation, are the Brothers of the Holy Grail."

In this passage, weighty with solemn secrets, we can perhaps catch a glimpse of that holy and momentous background out of which, in the 8th century, Charibert von Laon's Fellowship of the Holy Grail was born.

In a later incarnation Charibert himself carried the impulse of this Fellowship further in a new form when he returned to earth as Christian Rosenkreutz; Ernst Uehli, in *A New Quest of the Grail*, speaks of Rosicrucianism as "a Grail renewing." In Rosicrucianism the Grail Impulse lived in the hearts of simple and devoted men; in the Fellowship of the Holy Grail it had manifested through the deeds of those of Europe's new-born royal houses which married into Charibert's line.

In the working of the Grail Impulse through this fellowship, descent through the female line was as important as descent through the male. The Grail Maiden had her part to play as well as the Grail Knight. As Trevrizent explains to Parzival in Wolfram's epic: "Wherever a land is left lordless, if the people pray for a lord to be sent them from the Grail, that prayer is granted. God sends the men forth secretly; but the maids are openly bestowed in marriage, that their fruit may be gathered back into the Grail's service."

Charibert had a daughter Berta, who married Pippin II; through Berta the Grail Impulse descended to their son Charlemagne, whose greatgrand-daughter Judith was the mother of Alfred the Great. Through her the Grail Impulse came to England and united here with the Arthurian element then on the throne of Wessex, and later, in Alfred's grandson, Athelstan, on the throne of England itself. Through Athelstan's five beautiful sisters – Eadgitha, Elfgifa, Edgyfu, Elgive and Eadhilda – a new Grail Impulse born in England was carried back to the Continent and propagated there.

"Saxons, Jutes and Angles," says W. J. Stein, "created

in England forms of social life which in the ninth and tenth centuries worked back on the Continent and there reformed economic life. The Saxons contributed the forms of organisation proper to a trading and economic life; the Jutes and Angles the inner feeling for it; the Celts the spiritual background. What was thus prepared on the soil of England was a ferment destined to nourish Europe and the entire world for a long time to come." The medieval picturing of this is given in saga-form in the Grail legend of *Lohengrin*.

An entry in the Anglo-Saxon Chronicle in the year 921 records a newly discovered method of building defences with walls of rock. Out of this grew a new phase – the Lohengrin phase – of European history. For out of this grew the city-culture of the last thousand years.

It is not for nothing that the Lohengrin legend introduces Henry the Fowler. For he is also known as Henry the Town-Planner; and it was while he was Emperor of Germany that the seeds of this new city-culture spread from England and took root in Western Europe.

These seeds were carried by the five Anglo-Saxon princesses, all, through Alfred the Great, descendents of Charibert, who married into the leading European dynasties. Their relative, Prince Turketal, the founder of this new city-culture, conducted all five to their respective bridegrooms.

We have seen already how, in Wolfram's epic, *Parzival*, Klingsor had a historical prototype. The historical prototype of the Swan-Knight Lohengrin in the same epic was the Anglo-Saxon Prince Turketal, High Chancellor of England, grandson of Alfred the Great.

Prince Ethelward, Turketal's father, dies in the year
920. It was in the year following Turketal's succession
to his inheritance that the new method of defence
recorded in the Anglo-Saxon Chronicle sprang into
being. His uncle, King Edward the Town-Founder, and
his aunt, the intrepid Queen Ethelfleda of Mercia, took
up his idea with enthusiasm, building walled towns as
focal points of defence against the unceasing waves of
marauding Danes. Ethelfleda's Mound, from which the
mighty Warwick Castle was later to develop, is still in
existence as a reminder of these first beginnings.
When King Edward the Town-Founder appointed his
nephew Turketal High Chancellor, it is recorded that
he expressly placed in his hands "all negotiations, both
temporal *and spiritual*." This is reflected in King
Edward's laws.Walled towns having been established,
it was now enacted that all trade was to be transacted
within the safety of the city gates. Thus were laid down
the foundations of a new social and economic order,
with its roots in towns as commercial centres, bringing
quite new cultural developments in its train.
When King Edward the Town-Founder died in 924, his
son Athelstan came to the throne of Wessex. Athelstan
was a quite special being. He was a true Arthur-figure,
carrying forward this island's evolution through new
developments in accordance with the demands of an
emerging destiny. Between him and his cousin Turketal
there was a marriage of true minds.
Alfred the Great, aware of his grandson Athelstan's
special quality, knighted him while he was still a boy,
giving him "a scarlet cloak, a belt studded with
diamonds, and a saxon sword with a gold scabbard."
The boy was brought up at the Court of his aunt,
Queen Ethelfleda, who was dedicated to the same ideals

As Athelstan and Turketal, her nephews.

Under Athelstan all the Anglo-Saxon kingdoms were united for the first time. This was a result of the famous battle of Brunanburgh, fought in 937 against a devastating horde of Danes and Norsemen, Northumbrians and Scots, under the great Viking leader, Anlaf. Blood flowed, say the chronicles, from the rise of the sun to its setting; and among the enemy leaders, Constantine, King of the Scots, five Viking kings and seven Danish earls were all slain. Turketal fought in this battle at the head of the Mercian Division – his aunt Queen Ethelfleda's man – and would have been slain by Constantine had not one of his own men, Singinus, rushed to his aid and slain the King of the Scots first. Then we would have lacked the legend of Lohengrin; evolution would have had by some detour to achieve the step that legend presents pictorially.

This battle which so decisively united and consolidated England under Athelstan also opened the door to the next step in the spiritual plan for that time – the sowing on the Continent of England's new seed of city-culture. For Ingulph the historian tells us:

"When the news of the victory of Brunanburg spread throughout that whole Christian world, all the kings of the earth desired to contract friendly relations with Athelstan and all sent ambassadors to solicit the hands of the royal princesses of England."

So now began Prince Turketal's next mission – that of escorting the princesses to the different Courts of Europe, and with them the spiritual blueprints of his new walled commercial towns.

The situation on the Continent was fundamentally the same as in England. While here civilisation had been threatened by the open floodgates of the Danes, there it was the Hungarians who threatened to submerge the still-young Christian culture. Thus it is in keeping both with the outer historical situation and the supersensible situation underlying it that Wagner, in his opera, *Lohengrin*, makes Henry the Fowler arrive in Brabant at th crucial moment for the primary purpose of levying a force to fight against the Hungarian invaders.

It is to Henry the Fowler's Court that Prince Turketal conducts his first two princesses, the seventeen-year-old Eadgitha and her younger sister, Elfgifa, for the Emperor's son, Otto, to choose between them. Otto fell in love at first sight with Eadgitha, and the Duke of Burgundy with Elfgifa. The medieval poem *Lohengrin* describes this voyage of Turketal with the two English princesses up the Rhine to Cologne, referring to him quite openly under his Grail Mystery-name. Turketal, fighting at the Emperor's side now helps repulse the invading Hungarians in Europe as he had previously helped to repulse the invading Danes in England. Edgyfu had next to be conducted to the Court of Charles III, and Elgive to that of Ludwig of Aquitania. The youngest, Eadhilda, was also the most beautiful. She was wooed and won by Hugo of France; and William of Malmsbury gratefully records the many holy relics and other precious gifts sent to Athelstan in furtherance of her and her sisters' wooings and presented by him to the Abbey at Malmsbury, the Court-city in Athelstan's time – among the, "fleet horses, champing golden bits, the sword of Constantine the Great; the spear of Charlemagne, said also to have pierced our Saviour's side; a dazzling diadem; a portion of the Holy

Cross; a portion of the Crown of Thorns." When we remember how deeply holy relics were revered and how powerfully they worked into the soul-life of those times, we realise that the gifts connected with the Mystery of Golgotha were, both to donor and to recipient, gifts precious beyond price, and that the mission in connection with which they were offered must have been considered correspondingly so.

When Edmund succeeded Athelstan, and Edred in turn succeeded Edmund, Turketal still remained High Chancellor. During four reigns – Edward, Athelstan, Edmund, Edred – he filled this office. Then he begged to be allowed to relinquish it and to retire into monastic life as Abbot of Croyland. When in 975, he died, he had lived through six reigns and had seen the new city-culture firmly established.

At the end of his great poem, *Parzival*, Wolfram von Eschenbach tell briefly the story of Lohengrin. At first sight it seems an inartistic addition – a précis added as an extraneous pendant to the complicated and long-drawn-out epic of one soul's quest and its consummation. But as one muses on it, one sees that spiritually it belongs to the wholescope of the poem. Parzival achieves the Kingship of the Grail, and the little cameo of Lohengrin at the end indicates how the future builds further on his achievement.

In Wolfram's epic Lohengrin is the son of Parzival; but neither he nor we hear of him till almost the end of the epic, when Kundry brings the joyful news:

"The inscription on the Grail is read. You shall be lord thereof. Condwiramur your wife and your son Lohengrin to share that honour are elected too."

Now Parzival learns for the first time, and we with him, that he has two small sons, Kardeis and Lohengrin, twins born since he left Condwiramur his wife nearly five years ago. He gives God humble and joyful thanks. "If I have children, and my wife, too, God has dealt well with me indeed."

With Kundry as guide, Parzival and his black-and-white brother Fierifis ride to Montsalvat, where Parzival asks the healing question which makes the sick Amfortas whole again. Then Parzival rides on through the night to the "field full of tents and banners" in which his wife is lodged, reaching it at daybreak. She is in bed, asleep, with a small naked boy each side of her. Her old uncle Kyot flings back the coverlet, bidding her awake to joy. She leaps out of bed into Parzival's arms.

"I am told." said Wolfram, "that they kissed each other."

Kardeis, the elder twin, "The kingdom's heir, is crowned king, and two small hands bestowed broad lands in fee. When they had eaten bread, Duke Kyot and the nobles of Brobarz set out for home with their small king; the Templars, with Parzival, Condwiramur and Lohengrin, set out out for Montsalvat.

"It was late when they reached it. The castle was all lit up with a blaze of candles, as bright as though the whole forest were set on fire." So the little Lohengrin came to his future home.

Here Wolfram pauses and asks:

"Would you like to hear further?"

And then he appends to the sixteenth book of his long epic, *Parzival*, the little jewel, *Lohengrin*, which Rudolf Steiner tells us, "came to the fore as a Bavarian legend just at the time of the Meistersingers' contest on the Wartburg."

The story of Lohengrin is set in the tenth century, when Henry the Fowler was Emperor of Germany. Elsa, the young Duchess of Brabant, is being wooed against her will by her guardian, Duke Frederick, who has designs on her kingdom. Her young brother, Gottfried, who is her heir, mysteriously disappears. Duke Frederick accuses Elsa of having murdered him.

Henry the Fowler comes to Brabant, to judge the case. Unable to arrive at a verdict, he decrees that the judgement of God shall be sought in single combat.

On the day appointed, the whole city streams out to the lists. The Emperor bids the heralds sound the challenge. They do so; no knight appears to champion Elsa's cause. Again the trumpets sound; again silence follows.

A third time the trumpets sound; and now cries of wonder arise as a boat glides down the river, drawn by a snow-white swan, and in the boat a knight in shining armour.

"He stepped from his bark. The lady of the land gave him fair welcome. Rich and poor, who stood surrounding them, heard the words he spoke;

"'My lady duchess. If I hold lordship here, never enquire who I am. Only then can I remain with you; if you question me you must lose my love.'

"She pledged her oath as a woman to do his will."

Nobles from the Emperor's train pace out the duel-ground and draw its circle with their spear-tips. With his sword the Emperor strikes his shield thrice as it hangs on the Tree of Judgement. The two champions close in combat.

Duke Frederick falls, mortally wounded, confessing Elsa's innocence and his own guilt – it is he who had abducted Gottfried, who is later restored to his sister. The Swan-Knight is proclaimed victor and awarded Elsa's hand.

"After that, he held sway in Brabant. Wisely he judged, and many a knightly victory did he win. Fair children were born of the wedlock."

But the time came when Elsa could no longer stifle the fatal questions:

"Who are you? Whence do you come?"

Then sadly assembling the knights and citizens, the Swan-Knight revealed his secret:

"The Grail it was that sent me here to you. Its knight am I; my name is Lohengrin. And now I have unveiled my mystery, to the Grail I must return."

"There are many people in Brabant,"says Wolfram, "who remember how, when her questioning reft him from her, he parted thence. He was loth to leave her.

"But now his friend, the swan, came back with a small, trim boat, to fetch him home.

"He left three tokens behind him, a sword, a horn and a ring, then sailed away. Back over sea and land he passed to whence he came, to the land of his father Parzival, where the Grail held sway."

And then Wolfram cries in half-humourous exasperation; "Now why was the noble dame so wilful as to drive hence her dearest friend? He had warned her betimes not to question, when he came to her from the sea!"

Wolfram has brought us already, in the course of Parzival's story, rumours of such knightly services rendered by the Grail-band as these of Lohengrin; as, for example, when Trevrizent explains to Parzival:
"Wherever a land is left without its lord, then, if it be God's will and the people themselves desire it, one of the Grail-band is sent on an errand of mercy to be their lord and ruler."
Through such errands of mercy by members of the Grail-band new impulses are brought to earth to further human evolution. All such fresh impulses are carried down in the first place by initiates. The fresh impulse brought by the initiate known to us as Lohengrin is the foundation of the towns.
If we are to understand the legend, we have to look *through* its pictures to the spiritual realities underlying them. "We must always turn to legends," says Rudolf Steiner, "for enlightenment in regard to significant turning-points in evolution, for the truths they contain are deeper than those recorded in history. Legends show us how initiates intervene in the course of history; they are not to be regarded as accounts of happenings in the *outer* world."
Elsa, he tells us, is "the new form of consciousness, the civilisation of the middle classes." She can be thought of as the medieval soul grown ripe for the next great step in human evolution, the development of a city culture. It is important that this soul shall be united with the messenger who brings the seed of his new culture from Montsalvat, that is, from the spiritual worlds." Fair children were born from that wedlock."
But the delicate and highly elaborate work of the initiate, exoteric in that it is executed in the outer world, but esoteric in that is springs from secret divine sources,

must not be fingered or spied upon by mere human Curiosity. The silence of the spiritual worlds on arcane matters must be respected. What the initiate brings is to be regarded as a gift bestowed by those worlds.

In the physical world the initiate who brings the gift is, in an occult sense, a homeless man. His physical body is merely an instrument placed at the service of those higher ends he serves, is, merely the boat in which he is borne by the swan of his purified etheric sheath to the place where his mission awaits him.

The walling of the towns had been for defence; but the repercussions of those walls on the social and economic conditions of tenth century life were stupendous. Till then, what art and culture there was had been fostered in the monasteries; in the castles there had been lavish abundance and crude splendour; but the villein, under pressure from two masters, quite literally could not call his life his own.

But now, within the walled town, barter gave way to trade; the crafts and craftsmanship flourished, life could be lived with a modicum of safety; and – most precious of all – life could be lived with a modicum of liberty.

Within these walls there developed a new kind of community, based neither on the blood-tie nor on the feudal relationships of the great rural estates but on a comradeship of craftsmen. When we look back to the dignity and importance of the medieval guilds – for example, to the free masons who built our incredible Gothic cathedrals and developed into an arcane power behind the scenes – we realise what a tremendous step towards the unfettered unfolding of the human personality the foundation of the walled town was.

And more than this, Rudolf Steiner has said that in the founding of towns all over Europe the great mission of Christianity in the Middle Ages is expressed. "The task of the brotherhoods was so to fashion the world that it became a garment for the spirit – The Freemasons wanted nothing less than a contract with the priesthood in order so to mould external life that it could be an image of the whole structure of the world. A Gothic cathedral was built thus according to an idea that embraces far more than does the Cathedral itself. The divine life must stream in as a unity, like sunlight through the many-coloured panes of the cathedral windows."

"Spiritual life," says Rudolf Steiner again, "does not originate in material progress; but real spiritual progress is to be found where economic development is neither oppressed nor limited. Thus an abundant civilisation arose in the cities."

He speaks with great enthusiasm of the material and cultural achievements which had their beginnings in the towns – the art of printing, modern science, the universities. "The work of men like Copernicus, Kepler, Newton, would have been impossible without this city culture. Dante's *Divine Comedy* and the painters of the Renaissance grew out of it.

And then:

"This progress which came about in the Middle Ages is described in legendary form in the transition from Parsifal to Lohengrin."

Lohengrin's city culture has lasted a thousand years. It has grown ripe; it has grown over-ripe. It has helped to bring about the free unfolding of the individuality. But now "the last stage of Christianity, of which Lohengrin was the peak," says Steiner, "has degenerated into utilitarianism."

"Materialism," he continues, "must be superseded by a new phase, a new cycle. It is this phase that Anthroposophy asks to introduce."

And then he makes this momentous announcement:

"Anthroposophy is the successor of the movements of Parsifal and Lohengrin."

What does this mean? If every new impulse in human evolution is brought down to earth by an initiate, it must surely mean that Lohengrin's successor has already followed him, that the gift brought by Lohengrin's successor is already with us. It must surely mean that Anthroposophy is that new impulse.

It must surely mean that, just as Elsa of Brabant was the medieval soul, ripe for quickening by that last great impulse, so we, if we will, have it in our destinies to be the modern soul, ripe for quickening by this new one.

May fair children be born of this wedlock.

REFERENCES

Flor and Blanchefleur, Conrad Fleck
The Ninth Century, (Temple Lodge Press) W. J. Stein

LECTURES by RUDOLF STEINER:

Richard Wagner and Mysticism,
  Nurnberg, 2 Dec. 1907. "Anthroposophy Vol. 5 No. 2".

Parsifal and Lohengrin,
  Cologne, 3 Dec. 1905 – (Typed) See Z 212.

Richard Wagner in the Light of Anthroposophy,
  Berlin, 28 Mar. – 19 May 1905 (NSL 175-8).

The European Mysteries and their Initiates,
  Berlin, 6 May 1909. Anthroposophical Quarterly 1964.
  Vol. 9 No. 1.

A History of the Middle Ages,
  Berlin, 18 Oct. – 20 Dec. 1904. See 88/89.

Concerning the Temple Lost and Rediscovered,
  see "The Temple Legend" (R. Steiner Press).
  Berlin, 15 May – 5 June 1095.

Spiritual Bells of Easter,
  Cologne, 10, 11, Apr. 1909 in "The Festivals and their
  Meaning" (R. Steiner Press).

CHAPTER IX

THE PRINCESS AND THE TIN-TRADER

It is said that, in the period of persecution which followed Christ's Resurrection and Ascension, Joseph of Arimathea came with eleven disciples to the Isle of Avalon, and found on its lower slopes a sacred Druid spring, oriented towards the Midsummer sunrise. It is said that about it they built a circle of twelve huts, and dwelt and taught and baptised there, so that this spring became the heart of the first Christian settlement in Celtic Britain and it was in its healing waters that the first converts to what was to become the forerunner of Celtic Christianity were immersed. It is further said that it was in the spring, as in a hidden sanctuary, that Joseph placed the Holy Grail for safety, turning its waters red.

Legends bring us intimations of the spiritual happenings which underlie recorded history. They couch this news in a picture-language no longer transparent to our modern intellect but only to our musing hearts. How does the musing heart decipher this picture of Joseph secreting the Holy Grail at Avalon?

The Gospels tell of Joseph that he took down the Body of Christ from the cross and laid it in the virgin tomb prepared for his own body. Early Christian tradition tells of Joseph that he stood beneath the cross and received into the Cup of the Last Supper the blood

which gushed forth from the lance-wound in Christ's
side. We see him thus receiving both the Body and the
Blood of Christ in a fashion unshared by any other man
except, in a lesser degree by Nicodemus. These two
alone in all the world receive the Eucharistic Elements
in cosmic prototype.

When in the twelfth century, the legend of the Grail
becomes exoteric and is carried by trouvères from castle
to castle across Europe, these versions which are of
French as distinct from Germanic provenance all portray Joseph as the first Christian Guardian of the Grail,
and all hint that by this more is implied than is directly
said.

Thus, in the *Quest del Saint Graal* (written by Walter
Map some time before 1200), when Joseph, borne by
angels brings the ark containing the Grail to Galahad,
he is "clad as the first bishop of Christendom." Later,
also, in Malory's *Morte d'Arthur* (written in 1467, first
printed – by Caxton – in 1485) "it seemed that he had
in the midst of his forehead letters that said: *Se ye here
Joseph, the first bishop of Christendom.*" And in the Didot
Perceval (about 1220), Merlin tells Arthur that not only
was the Grail given into Joseph's keeping by Christ
Himself, but that from the cross He also gave into
Joseph's keeping certain secret words.

In Sire Robert de Borron's *Romanz de l'historie du Graal*
(written in 1190), Christ teaches these secret words to
Joseph, telling him that for the love Joseph had towards
Him he shall have this symbol of Christ's death and
that all who see it shall be of Christ's company.
Joseph's brother-in-law, Brons, has a son Alain, who is

to go westward to the *Vaux d'Avaron* (the Vale of
Avalon), and whose own son will be worthy to become
Guardian of the Grail. "Tell Brons," says Christ,
"how God did communicate with thee the Holy Words,
which are sweet and precious and gracious and piteous,
which are properly called and named the Secret of the
Grail."

When Alain's son comes to Brons and receives the
Grail, "then shall the meaning of the doctrine of the
Holy Trinity be made known."

In his *Early History of Merlin*, de Borron speaks again of
the great love between Christ and Joseph; when Pilate
there gives the Grail to Joseph, he remarks; "Much hast
thou loved this man," and Joseph replies: "Thou hast
said truly." One is reminded of the description of John
in his own Gospel as the disciple whom Jesus loved, a
phrase which is not limited to the sphere of feelings but
indicates also that to this disciple deeper teachings were
committed than to the others.

Out of all this the figure of Joseph emerges as that of an
Initiate into whose care Christ has confided deeper and
more esoteric truths concerning the consequences of His
Passion and Death than those incorporated in the
exoteric dogmas of Holy Church. Only to those who
were worthy could these deeper truths be imparted; a
Galahad could achieve the Quest of the Grail, but not a
Lancelot or Gawain. So there sprang from Joseph an
esoteric stream of historical Christianity, in a hidden
way interpenetrating and revivifying it.

But there came a period of decline into spiritual darkness. The intellect and materialism held sway. The

Grail withdrew, and the benediction of its blessed visitation ceased.

Malory describes its recession thus:

"They saw come from heaven a hand, but they saw not the body, and then it came right to the Vessel and took it, and the Spear, and so bore it up to heaven. Since then was there never no man so hardy for to say that he had seen the Sancgreal."

Other tellings of this story of the Grail describe its withdrawal under other images. In Albrecht von Scharfenberg's *Titurel* (written in 1270) its retreat is in the land of Prester John. In other versions it is taken into the custody of angels. In the Glastonbury legend Joseph lays it in the sanctuary of the Chalice Well.

But its seclusion will not last forever. It has withdrawn to its own place to bide its time. In the new age which will arise with the moving of the sun into the next constellation, the contents of the Grail, its power renewed, will be openly united with the contents of historical Christianity. Already today, in preparation for the time, Joseph brings forth again the chalice from the well. Anthroposophy today prepares us to be the preparers of that union.

In Cornish folk-lore, Joseph of Arimathea is said to have been the son of a Celtic princess, Rhiernwylydd, and of her husband, Bicanys, a Phoenician tin-trader living at Land's End. How are we to understand this surprising genealogy?

We know that it was the particular mission of Jewry to prepare the physical body in which the Word was to be made flesh, and that, in dedication to this mission, for

long centuries the Hebrew bloodstream had been kept
pure and unpolluted by foreign infiltration. Even within
this guarded racial bloodstream, certain marriages were
arranged by the spiritual leader of the people, in order
to produce a socially favourable line of physical heredity for the promised Messiah. To arrange and to watch
over such marriages was, indeed, one of the esoteric
functions of the Essenes.

The legend of the aged Joseph being marked out to be
Mary's husband by the budding of his rod in the Temple is a picture of such a spiritually directed choice; and
in both St. Luke and St. Matthew great emphasis is laid
on the genealogy of the Jesus Child, the latter giving it
in detail back to Abraham, the former back to God.

It is also with good reason that Jesus is so often called
in the Gospels, Jesus of Nazareth. For Nazareth was a
colony founded by Nezer, one of the five close disciples
of the great Eddene leader a century earlier, Jeschu
ben Pandira, that Bodhisattva whose great destiny it is
to become the Maitreya Buddha in far centuries
to come. Nezer means "branch", and refers to the Tree of
Jesse. For Nazareth was a place devoted to the dedication of the forces of heredity to the creation of the most
humanly possible perfect body for the Messiah; the
name, Jesus of Nazareth, told the initiated that Jesus
was of a specially chosen line within the Chosen People.
Against this background it is clear that the tradition of
Joseph of Arimathea's Celtic-Phoenician ancestry is not
meant to be taken literally, but to be indicating, in a
picture, preparations for the looked-for Incarnation
made by Phoenicia and by Celtica on other levels and
in other spheres.

If we examine the father-stream of Bicanys in this light, what do we find?

Not only had the Hebrew blood-stream been kept pure of foreign infiltration for its high purpose, but all its formative forces had also been husbanded to that same end – none had to be diverted to the arts, to architecture, sculpture, painting.

So,when the time came for the building of Solomon's Temple, he had to call upon a helper whose blood-stream had not been kept pure. Hiram was a widow's son (that is, an Initiate); his mother was of the tribe of Naphtali; but his father, a worker in brass, was a man of Tyre. It was a *Phoencian* who built that Temple which, says Rudolf Steiner, "was to be created outwardly until in Christ-Jesus appeared the Being who could build it anew in three days."

When Wolfram von Eschenbach, in his *Parzival*, tells us that it is on the Grail-stone that the Phoenix dies and is re-born, he is telling us of a process of death and resurrection, both in Man and in the Earth, connected with the Grail-forces. The Mysteries of the Phoenix – the Mysteries of Death and Resurrection – born in Sheba, had their home in Phoenicia (hence the latter's name), notably at Tyre, its mother-city.

Coins of ancient Tyre bear a serpent winding round an egg, and beside it a date-palm standing. This egg, which bears within it the diaphanous state of matter of both a past and a future period of world-evolution, was Wolfram's Grail-stone in another image. The date-palm, *Phoenix dactylifera*, was in Phoenicia the tree in which the Phoenix died and was reborn, and was itself, with new feathery branches shooting from the centre while old ones died into bark below, a symbol of death and resurrection.

It was known from the dimmest ages of antiquity that it was at Tyre that the greatest treasure in the world was to be preserved until the time was ripe for it to enter the stream of earthly evolution. Because of this, the city had had to be founded in a spot having special connections with supersensible worlds. Nonnus, in his *Dionysiaca*, tells how Herakles sent messengers in search of "a flaming tree growing on ambrosial rocks, a snake curled round its trunk, and on its topmost boughs an eagle bearing a well-wrought bowl." This was to be the site of the Temple of Herakles; Tyre was to be built around it. What, then, was this greatest treasure of the ancient world?

Legend tells of how, at the War in Heaven, Lucifer wore a crown of sixty thousand brilliant jewels. The fairest, a pure emerald, Michael's sword struck from the crown, and it fell from Heaven to Earth, where it shone unseen in a secret sea-cave till the Phoenicians found it and fashioned it into a wonderful emerald dish. Placed in the Temple of Herakles at Tyre, it shone miraculously by night for many centuries, till, when Hiram was King of Tyre, he gave it to Balkis, the Queen of Sheba, on her way to visit King Solomon.

Balkis had loved Hiram until she met Solomon and found him "beautiful as a statue of gold and ivory." As a token of her love, she gave the miraculous emerald dish to him. After the building of the Temple it was preserved there till it passed into the keeping of the Essenes, in whose Upper Room Christ filled it with the solemn wine of the Last Supper. And two days later, at the taking down of the Body from the Cross, Joseph of Arimathea again received into it the precious wine of Christ's Blood.

We are told that when the Temple was finished, it

shone supersensibly like a star. The emerald Grail which shone by night shone henceforth not at Tyre but at Jerusalem, guiding to chosen parents souls whose task was to help to prepare the right stream of heredity for the Incarnation of the Word when the time for this was due.

So we become aware of both Phoenix-stream and Grail-stream in the father-stream of Bicanys. And this pagan Phoenicia had still a further gift to offer Christianity.

Greek mythology tells us that Europa was the daughter of Phoenix, King of Sidon, Tyre's sister-city. (Homer calls her the daughter of the Phoenix itself). During the time of the Egyptian civilisation, Jupiter, in the form of a bull, carried her to Crete, the Kingdom of Minos (whose name means "intelligence"), the birthplace of European culture. We can see portrayed in this myth an impulse which took its rise in Phoenicia – the descent from the more supersensible dream-consciousness of Asia to the day-waking consciousness of Europe, born of the developing intellect.

Egyptian mythology portrays the same descent in a different picture, it was at Biblos in Phoenicia that Isis found the coffin of Osiris. While Osiris lived, men still retained the old pictorial consciousness; when Typhon cut the body of Osiris into fourteen pieces, that consciousness was broken up. From Phoenicia came the fourteen letters of the abstract alphabet.

It was Pherekydes of Syros, initiated in Phoenicia, who became the first Greek philosopher, building a bridge from the old perceptual to the new conceptual thinking. And it was his Tyrian pupil, Pythagoras, who built a similar bridge by means of mathematics.

So we see Phoenicia inaugurating the European culture

of which Greece was the first and the most glorious flower.

Clement of Alexandria, the Early Church Father of the second century A.D., who founded the first Christian philosophy, spoke of two streams of preparation for Christianity – that of Moses and the prophets; and that of the Greek philosophers. Moses and the Prophets educated a race to prepare the body for the Christ; the Greek philosophers developed for the Western world a mode of thinking which could comprehend Him. It was actually from Ephesus where St. John had found inspiration in Greek philosophy, that the esoteric Christianity of the Grail came to the West.

Since all this had its roots in Phoenicia, we need no longer be surprised that Bicanys is characterised as a Phoenician, nor that he is a tin-trader, nor that he lives at Land's End. For with tin is associated the activating of the fore-brain, the seat of conceptual thinking; and it was for tin from the tin-mines of Cornwall that history tells us Phoenician ships made stealthy and mysterious voyages to the West.

The belief in Joseph of Arimathea's visits to Cornwall, which has survived among Cornish folk until nearly two thousand years after his death, associated him with the Cornish tin-mines; within living memory Cornish children still chanted a carol, "St. Joseph was a tin-merchant, a tin-merchant, a tin-merchant;" and the tinsmiths still blessed a certain stage in their craft with a whispered rune, "Joseph was in the tin-trade."

The Latin Vulgate's description of Joseph as *nobilis decurio* is translated in our English Authorised Version as "an honourable counsellor", St. Jerome, so much nearer in time to traditions now growing moribund, translates the same phrase as minister of mines."

When tin was mixed with copper, the bronze age dawned, with its clearer consciousness, and its control of the will and the feeling-life. The bull is a picture of the will; out of this learning to control the will arose the slaying of the Minotaur, the Mithraic rites of initiation, the bull-dancing of Crete. Even the bull-fights held in modern Spain could be regarded as having their origin in the racial memories of that era.

We see then how important tin was at a certain point for the whole course of mankind's future evolution, and why, and that the fact that Britain was a tin-island was of immense significance to the civilisation of the East.

In the Gilgamesh epic, for example, we find this culture-hero, born into the Copper Age, going westward to Burgenland, and there meeting Upnapisham, a great Initiate from the tin-island of Britain, and from him receiving the impulse to bring a Bronze culture into being in his own land.

The Christ descended into an earthly body during the Greco-Roman epoch, that is, during the Iron Age which succeeded the bronze one. While Arthurian literature is for the most part fashioned in terms of the courtly chivalry and knightly striving of Christian times, the content of the King Arthur legend, as Rudolf Steiner tells us," goes back to a very early epoch," and here and there in it we find atavistic echoes, such as the Addanc and the one-eyed Woodward of Broceliande.

Such an atavistic echo occurs in the story of the Castle of Copper in *Perceval li Gallois*:

"Perceval comes to the Castle of Copper, whose folk worshipped the bull of copper and believed not in any other God."

"The bull of copper was in the midst of the castle, upon four columns of copper. It bellowed so loud at all hours of the day that it was heard for a league all round about; and within the bull there was an evil spirit that gave answers concerning whatsoever any should ask of it.

"At the gateway were two men made of copper by the art of nigromancy. They held two great mallets of iron; and so strongly they struck that nought mortal is there in the world that might pass through.

"As Perceval cometh nigh, a Voice cried aloud above the gate that no power had the sergeants of copper to harm such a knight as he. They hold their mallets quite still, and he entereth the castle, where he findeth great plenty of folk, which all were misbelievers.

"The Voice warneth him to make them all pass through the gateway, to prove which are willing to believe in God. Of one thousand and five hundred, but thirteen were not slain of the iron mallets. The thirteen had firmly bound their belief in our Lord.

"The evil spirit that was in the bull of copper issued forth thereof as it had been lightning, and the bull of copper melted all in a heap. The thirteen that remained sent for a hermit of the forest, and so made themselves be held up and baptised.

"Then they scattered themselves and made hermitages among strange forests."

The number saved is the number that sat at the table of the Last Supper; the number that sat at Galahad's last meal at Carbonek; the number of those shared the fiery baptism of Pentecost; the mystic thirteen of the Rosicrucian Brotherhoods. The scene is like a small, apocalyptic prophecy of that separation of the sheep from the goats which will begin already in the next – the sixth – epoch. In de Borron's *Small Holy Grail* (1190), a second prophetic foretaste of that separation occurs during Joseph of Arimathea's journey from the East to England.

Famine had fallen on the band accompanying Joseph. At Christ's direction, he sent out Brons, his brother-in-law, to catch a fish, which, again at Christ's direction, he places on the table beside the Cup he carries with him.

When Joseph's companions were called to the table, "All who were pure of heart were filled with the rare sweetness of the world, to that they could neither conceive nor desire anything beyond it." Others experienced nothing.

Peter, one of Joseph's followers, remarked:

"'Then ye are the guilty ones who have caused our famine.'

"Those who were shut out asked Peter what kind of a vessel it was that they had seen on the table.

"Peter said:

"'Through this vessel we were separated, through the virtue and the power which dwells in it. For it will allow no sinner to come near it.'

"They asked further:

"'What is this vessel called?'

"Peter answered:

"'He who wishes to call it by its right name calls it the Grail.'"

While the Grail Stream penetrated with profound

understanding the meaning of Christ's incarnations for men and for the Earth, the Arthur Stream (like the Mysteries of Hibernia from which it sprang and which had watched the descent of Christ through the spheres towards incarnation) directed its gaze to the Cosmic Christ, striving, by righting of wrongs and by rooting out evil customs, to bring His cosmic law and order into earthly culture, making the Round Table an image of the beautiful order of the heavens.

In his placing of the Fish beside the Cup upon his famine table, Joseph of Arimathea's is the human hand which first brings these two stream together in archetypal prophecy of when, eight hundred years later, they were to flow together in the ninth century over Europe.

"Out of the stone which fell from Lucifer's crown," says Rudolf Steiner, "was made the Holy Grail. The mutual fertilisation of these two evolutionary streams (Christ's and Lucifer's) began at the moment when the sacrificial blood of the Christ flowing from the Cross was received into the vessel of the Holy Grail and *brought to the West from the East*."

In this mighty migration, when Joseph of Arimathea brings the Grail to England and places it in the care of the Celtic Folk-Soul, Phoenician tin-trader, with all his infinitely rich endowments, is united with Celtic princess.

From about 3,000 B.C., when the Egyptian culture-epoch was at its height, the Celts had come westward in waves from beyond the Caucasus till they had covered all Europe north of the Alps, setting among and mingling with the more backward peoples they found there, consecrating their megaliths to higher spiritual purposes, and becoming their leaders and teachers.

When their mission of establishing the pre-Christian civilisation of North and Central Europe had been accomplished, later invasions from the East had gradually submerged them driving the survivors westward until, by that great turning-point of time at which the Christ came to earth, they still flourished as a race only along Europe's western borders.

Their Druidic Mysteries were established in places having a social connection with the ether-forces in and surrounding the Earth. Not only were the Druids, with the innate gifts of Celtic seership heightened by long years of training, able, with the help of their cromlechs, their megalithic circles such as Stonehenge, their great stone alignments such as those at Carnac, to read in the interplay of sun and shadow how rightly to guide the people, but in such spiritual sensitive regions they were also able to see supersensible events painted, as it were, upon the ether.

Clement of Alexandria reminds us that Christ already existed before he appeared on Earth, that he existed then in spheres beyond the Earth, and that it was from these spiritual worlds that he has inspired men in the Ancient Mysteries.

In the sanctuaries of the Druidic Mysteries, there came a high moment when the doubts and difficulties which were part of the discipline of their path of Initiation were resolved by the appearance of an exalted Cosmic Being. This Cosmic Being they recognised, through their own connection with the etheric regions, when, as the Christ descended towards His earthly incarnation, He entered the sphere of the airy realms mantling the Earth. There He became for them the King of the Elements.

Not only was the Christ's passage through the sphere of ether-forces visible to the Druids; but through the disturbance of that sphere by the earthquake and the eclipse of the sun which the Gospels record as taking place on the first Good Friday, they were even able to participate in vision in the Crucifixion on Golgotha itself.

"Ye have heard much of Joseph of Arimathie," says the *Morte d'Arthur*, "how he was sent by Jesu Christ into this land for to teach and preach the holy Christian faith." When he reached "this land", in what mood and into what religious climate can one envisage the message being received by such as had been eye-witnesses of the Event of which he brought earthly tidings?

We know how what the Grail legends call "the New Law" was received elsewhere among the Celts. In regions where the Druidic culture had declined – and it is such decadence that the Latin writers one-sidedly described – Christianity was opposed. But where it had remained pure, the Druids were already liegemen to the cosmic Christ even before the teachings of the incarnated Christ reached them.

Joseph then would find himself among a people of all the peoples in the world the least resistant to conversion. The Celts did not think of Christianity as superseding Druidism but as fulfilling it. The Druids themselves found nothing strange in becoming the first Celtic priests and still remaining Druids.

To the contemplative eye the Grail legends themselves

are not wanting in delicately veiled allusions to this supersensible participation in the Events of Palestine. In *Percival li Gallois* the Master of the Knights speaks as a Celtic Initiate:

"I saw the Grail, saith the Master, or ever Joseph collected therein the blood of Jesus Christ."

In *The Prose Percival* the old Christian priest speaks as one who has been and may well still be a Druid:

"*Je vi li Graal avant que li Rois Perchieres Joseph, qui ses onques fu, recuilli le sanc Jesu-Crist.*"

And in *Perlesvaux*, when the Grail hero comes to the Isle of the Ageless Elders, the two men with white beards and young faces rise and adore his shield, which had been Joseph of Arimathea's.

"Sir," they say to him, "marvel not at what we do, for we knew well the knight who bore this shield before you. We saw him many times before God was crucified."

Out of the Druidic supersensible perceptions of the descending Christ came Celtic Christianity's experience of Him in His cosmic aspect. The very gifts the Greeks had had to lose in order to inaugurate a mode of thinking that would apprehend Christ incarnated in a human body, these very gifts were the ones that Celts had to keep in order to perceive the Christ as a spiritual Being. The Greeks had to develop an understanding of earthly Christianity, the Celts of cosmic Christianity.

When the Greeks had fulfilled this mission, their greatness declined. Their Folk-Soul withdrew, renouncing further advancement in order to become the spiritual guardian of exoteric Christianity.

When the Celts had fulfilled their parallel mission, their greatness also declined. Their Folk-Soul also withdrew also renouncing further advancement, in order to become the spiritual guardian of esoteric Christianity, especially as now carried by the united Grail and Arthurian streams.

There were dark days ahead in which, in order that man might feel completely at home on the earth, it became necessary for him to be cut off from the cosmos. In the face of such development, Celtic Christianity was to prove "too bright and good for human nature's daily food."

From the middle of the fifth century onwards, waves of Anglo-Saxon invasion brought with them into England an infiltration of the old Germanic gods.

Alongside these, Celtic Christianity survived among the conquered Britons. It was not their pagan conquerors, but another stream of Christianity drawn to England by this paganism, which dealt Celtic Christianity its death-wound.

Under the year 596, the *Anglo-Saxon Chronicle* records: "In this year Pope Gregory sent Augustine to England with a good number of monks, who preached God's word to the English people."

In the following year, one week after St. Augustine had received King Aethelbert of Kent into the Roman Church, St. Columba, the great missionary of the Celtic Church, died on Iona. It was like a prophetic picture of what was to follow.

For a time the two Churches existed side by side; but as the Roman Church increased in numbers and power, co-existence grew more and more uneasy. Matters came to a head when King Oswiu of Northumbria, who had been converted by monks from Iona, married a princess from Kent, who brought with her her own Roman chaplain, so that the King found himself celebrating Easter while the Queen was keeping Lent. In the year 644 the

King summoned the Synod of Whitby to try and solve these divergences.

These divergences were, indeed, symptomatic of the deep differences, in approach of the two streams. The Roman Easter Rule changes with each new Calendar; the Celtic clung to the cosmic reckoning which all Christendom had used up to the years 343. This cosmic approach to the Celtic Church speaks clearly in a letter written to the Pope by St. Columbanus of Bangor at the end of the sixth century:

"How can the victory of Christ over death, surely a word of the light, be celebrated on a day when the age of the moon is such that Darkness overcomes Light?"

Equally clearly speaks the new earthly logic when, the Roman priest, Wilfrid of York, having established that the Keys of Heaven had been given to St. Peter, King Oswiu decided in favour of Rome, explaining (as the Venerable Bede reports):

"I would not wish to have St. Peter as my enemy, lest, when I knock at heaven's gate, he should tell me, 'I shall not let you in.'"

So Celtic Christianity, fatally wounded, slowly pined away. But it has a Phoenix-nature.

When, at the Synod of Whitby, St. Colman of Lindisfarne said of the Celtic Easter Rule, "Our forefathers received it from John, the disciple whom the Lord loved," he was expressing a spiritual if not a literal fact. For Celtic Christianity was like a seed-picture of one aspect of the John-Christianity of the future, given to Western man to bury in his heart till its time becomes due.

Schelling speaks of the two streams of historical Christianity which have hitherto maintained their existence in the West – Roman Catholicism and Protestantism – as

the Peter-stream and the Paul-stream, and of the
Christianity of the future as the John-stream.

When the Greek archangel of historical Christianity and
the Celtic archangel of esoteric Christianity mingle their
streams, the two spiritual realities behind the symbols
of Phoenician tin-trader and Celtic princess will indeed,
as the Cornish folk-genealogy foreshadows, bring a ful-
ler understanding of the Grail committed to the keeping
of Joseph of Arimathea. Then the time of the John-
stream of Christianity will have come.

REFERENCES

Kings, VII, 13-14.
St. Mark, XV, 43.
Perceval li Gallois, (12th century).
Le Petit Saint Grail, Sire Robert de Borron
(13th century).

LECTURES by RUDOLF STEINER:

The East in the Light of the West,
   Munich, 23-31 Aug. 1909.

CHAPTER X

MERLIN IN WACE AND LAYAMON

Sir Thomas Malory, a "knight-prisoner" writing his *Morte d'Arthur* within the grim walls of Newgate Prison during the War of the Roses (he records that he finished it in 1470), introduces Merlin as one whose bizarre powers and ancestry are too well known to need comment or explanation.

When, in the early pages, Merlin explains to the kings "that boy Arthur's" claim to the throne, "some of them laughed him to scorn, as King Lot: and more other called him a witch." When later, in Arthur's first war, Merlin counsels discretion, King Lot again mocks him – "Be we well-advised to be feared of a dream-reader?" But as time goes on, Malory tells us that "all men had great marvel that any man has such great speed to come and go on earth as Merlin;" that "for the most part of the days of his life, Arthur was much ruled by the counsel of Merlin;" and that, in Arthur's later war with the eleven kings, "all the three kings and the whole barons said that Merlin said passingly well, and it was done anon as Merlin had devised."

But what Malory never explains is why the two conspirators preparing to poison Arthur warn each other: "Beware of Merlin, for he knoweth all things *by the devil's craft*"; why when Merlin falls in love with Nimue,

"She was afraid of him because *he was a devil's son*"; and why Sir Ewaine, when he prevents his mother, Morgan le Fay, from murdering his father, King Urience, cries out bitterly: "men say that *Merlin was begotten of a devil*; but I may say that an earthly devil bare me."

Yet, in the light of Rudolf Steiner's lectures, it is this sinister paternity which gives us the key to an understanding of Merlin's knowledge of the shape of things to come, and of his use of his own preternatural wisdom in fostering impulses rightly connected with evolution as it moves on towards the future.

In 1155, just over three centuries earlier than Malory had finished *Le Morte d'Arthur*, Wace had finish his *Roman de Brut*. In 1204, just over two and half centuries before Malory, Layamon had finished his *Brut*. Both recount the circumstances of Merlin's paternity in dramatic detail, set in a frame of English history which is not the English history we were taught at school, but which offers to the anthroposophical eye a kind of supersensible verity of its own.

Both Wace and Layamon were Churchmen, Wace Norman, Layamon Anglo-Saxon. Wace, born in Jersey in 1100, educated at Caen, a Canon of Bayeux, found such joy in the Arthurian stories that in his youth he went on a pilgrimage to the Forest of Broceliande. He reports regretfully that he found no fairies there!

He dedicated his *Roman de Brut* to Eleanor of Acquitaines, who had transformed the Anglo-Norman Court with her troubadours on the accession of her husband, Henry of Anjou, to the throne of England in 1154. Henry shared her devotion to the Grail and Arthurian stories, and an illumination from the *Mort Artu* shows him dictating to Walter Map "les auentures del Saint Graal." So much royal favour did the *Roman de*

Brut find that King Henry requested Wace to write a similar chronicle of the Norman Invasion of England. The *Roman de Rou*, completed in 1160 – only 94 years after the event – and interwoven with lively and picturesque details gathered by Wace from citizens of Rouen whose grandfathers had been eye-witnesses of Duke Williams preparations, was the result, as fascinating in the twentieth century as in the twelfth.

Layamon tells us that he himself is "a priest, living among the people at a noble church on the banks of the River Severn." (Arley Regis in North Worcestershire). He tells us that he took three noble books for his model, one in Anglo-Saxon by St. Bede, one in Latin by St. Augustine, and Wace's *Roman de Brut* in Norman-French. "Layamon took quills in his fingers," he tells us, "and set down the true words on book-skin, and condensed the three books into one." His *Brut*, written in the verse-form of contemporary minstrels, contains a prophecy even truer than he could have anticipated – "Of Arthur shall gleemen sing gloriously."

Both chroniclers bring Merlin into being and into action at that arcane turning-point in English history when the struggle between native Briton and encroaching Anglo-Saxon takes a dramatic turn.

Vortigern, the Christian British King, has married Rowena, daughter of Hengist, the pagan Saxon chief. At Rowena's entreaty, Vortigern grants a love-day, on which five hundred Saxons and five hundred Britons are to meet weaponless and in peace.

They meet "in a plain that was pleasant beside the Abbey of Ambresbury," the Briton without weapons, but the Saxons "each with a long knife laid by his shank within his hose." They sat together in seeming amity till Hengist cried: "*Nimad covre saex!*" (Pluck forth your knives!). "In that place the most valiant lords of the kingdom were slain."

Hengist gripped Vortigern by the mantle, "and they bound him fast till he rendered to them freely of his cities and walled places. Not a turf of land did there remain to him in hand."

So he "fled beyond the Severn and passed deeply into Wales." He feared danger from two directions – on the one hand from Hengist and the Saxons; on the other from Ambrosie Aurelie and Uther, the two brothers of Constant, the British King whom he had slain and whose throne he had usurped. They had fled to Armorica (Brittany), but at any moment they might well return with an army of Little Britons.

His wise men advised him to build a mighty tower on the summit of Mount Snowdon, in which he could be safe from all these foes. A deep dyke was dug, and a wall was begun about it. But as much as was built each day collapsed by night.

After a "se'nnight" of this, Vortigern said to his wizards:

"By my faith, I wonder sorely what may be amiss with my tower, since the Earth will not endure it. Search and enquire the reason of this thing, and now these foundations shall be made sure."

The wizards went, "some to the woods and some to the cross-ways, and cast lots and sang incantations. For full three nights their crafts there they practiced." But all failed in their divining, except one, whose name was Joram. He reported:

"If there were found in any land any male-child that never had father, and opened his breast, and took of his blood, and mingled this with the lime that is in the wall, then would that wall stand till the world's end."

Vortigern sent out messengers, two by two, all over Wales, in search of such a child. "To and fro, high and low they sought and searched"; but nowhere could they find one.

At last two of the messengers came to a township called Caermerdin. (Today it is called Carmarthen, the name means "the seat of Merlin".) Weary, they rested for a moment, watching "the burgh-lads at play."

Two of the boys began to quarrel. One struck the other, shouting;

"Take that, you king's son!"

The other replied with disdain:

"A king's son I am, You, Merlin, are nobody's son. A father you never had!"

Then Vortigern's messenger rose and went into the burgh, and sought out Eli, its reve, and said to him:

"Send the young lad Merlin to the king in all haste, and his mother with him.

Eli led Merlin to the noble minister within the town walls, where his mother was "a hooded nun, of right holy life." He brought them together to King Vortigern.

"Good lady," said the king, "tell me, who was your father?"

And she told him:

"Daughter was I to Canaan, King of Dimetia. The third part of all this land stood in my father's hand."

"Lady," said King Vortigern again, "who was the father of Merlin, your son?"

She hung her head, and though a little while.

"King," she said, "when I was fifteen years of age, asleep in my bower, there came to me the fairest thing that was ever born. This I saw in dream each night. This thing, that glistened of gold, oft-times embraced me and came to me very nigh. When my time was come, this boy I had. I know not who begat him in this worlds-realm, whether it were evil-thing or on God's behalf dight. I know not any more to say of my son, how he came to the world."

Then Vortigern sent for Magan, a learned clerk. "From the beginning to the end, he told him all."

Then said Magan:

"In books I have found it written that a certain order of spirit, called Incubi, ranges between the moon and our earth. Their home and regions is the air, but this warm world is their resort. They know well how to clothe themselves in human shape. Merlin would be of such a being born."

Then Merlin asked:

"King, for what am I brought hither?"

And when he had heard, he cried:

"Let Joram come before me, and I will prove him liar."

When Joram was come, Merlin said:

"Tell me, Joram, why falleth this wall to the ground?"

Joram was still. He could not tell.

"King," said Merlin, "let the dyke be dug seven feet deeper, and you will come to a wondrous fair stone."

The dyke was dug seven feet deeper, and there-right they found the stone.

"Tell me, Joram," said Merlin, "What is beneath this stone?"

Joram was still. He could not tell.

"A water is here-under," Merlin told the King. "Do away the stone; the water you shall find."

They did away the stone; they found the water.

"Tell me, Joram," said Merlin, "what dwelleth in the water?"

Joram was still. He could not tell.

"Two strong dragons dwell there," said Merlin.

"Empty the pit of water, and you will find them, one milky-white, one red as blood."

They emptied the pit of water, and there came forth two dragons, one milk-white, and one as red as blood. Most fiercely did they fight each other, till the red dragon mortally wounded the white, and each returned to his hole.

"Each midnight they begin to fight," said Merlin. "It is through their fighting that the wall is fallen, and not for lack of my blood."

Then asked King Vortigern what these dragons betokened.

"They betoken kings yet to come," Merlin told him, "who would hold this realm in charge when you are gone from it."

"In what hour," asked King Vortigern,"shall I be gone from it?"

"That hour is at hand," said Merlin. "Already Aurelie and Uther have left Armorica, and now they sail speedily in the sea. Tomorrow will they come to the seastrand at Totnes. The Briton will make Aurelie their king; and after him Uther; and after Uther, Uther's son, a king most brave."

And even so it came to pass.

"When Ambrosie Aurelie had been made king, he went to Ambresbury, to kneel beside the graves of those foully slain at Hengist's love-day. It was in his mind to raise a monument to their worship. He asked counsel of the Archbishop of Caerleon as to how this might be done.

"We have a prophet, who is named Merlin," the Archbishop told him. "if any man might find him and bring him to you, he would give you the best counsel."

The king sent messengers far and wide over his kingdom, in search of Merlin, promising "both silver and gold" for his counsel.

Two of these knights came to Alaban, "a fair well in Welsh-land, much loved by Merlin, in which he often bathed." They found him sitting on "its strand", and give him the king's message.

"I reck not of his silver and his gold," Merlin replied. "If for such a thing I took care, my craft would go from me. Before yesterday noon I knew of your coming; had I so wished, you would not have found me. Aurelie the king and Uther, his brother – I knew them both ere they were born, though I have never seen either with eye. To the king I will come."

When these tidings came to King Aurelie, he rode out, and all his knights with him, to welcome Merlin. "the son of no man."

The king began to ask many things "of the world's course and of things to come." But Merlin told him:

"O Aurelie, if I made boast and game of these matters lightly among men, my spirit that is in my breast would wrath himself and become silent, and my wise words would foreclose. But whenever any need shall come to any of my people, and I may with my will dwell still, then may I say how it afterwards shall happen."

The dramatic bombast of the adolescent boy confronting Joram has matured into the responsible knowledge and self-knowledge of the adult seer." If for such things as gold and silver I took care, my craft would go from me ... if I made boast and game of these matters, my spirit that is in my breast would become silent, and my wise words would foreclose."

King Lot's epithet of "dream-reader" and "more other" knights' epithet of "witch" have clung too long to an exalted being who, rightly understood, we have cause to revere. When the Archbishop of Caerleon speaks of him as a "prophet", for a moment one is shaken. Then one recollects how Rudolf Steiner characterises prophecy, and one realises that in Merlin a being with this gift does indeed stand – nay, tower – before us.

When Steiner tells us that Nostradamus, gazing at the starry heavens, found "predictions rising in him in the form of strange pictures and imaginations," we are reminded of Merlin when the nights find him at his well – "then sate he still a long time, and then he spoke again." When Steiner tells us further that the prophet "needs tranquillity of soul", we are reminded of Merlin's words "when I may with my will stand still, then may I see how it afterwards shall happen." And when we note that it is "when any need shall come to any of my people" that Merlin exercises his gift, we become aware that he does this in full accord with what Steiner gives as the reason for prophecy – "that men do not go blindly on into the future but can set their goals and direct their impulses for the sake of evolution."

Layamon tells us that Merlin had already before they met found the answer to King Aurelie's problem of a monument to raise beside the graves of the slain Britons.

"Now will I counsel three of thy nearest need. I know a work with wonder accomplished; far the work stands, in Ireland. It is named the Giants' Ring. The stones of it are great; and as great is their virtue. There was never any man born who might with strength bring them thence."

"How might I then bring them hither?" asked the king. "It was said of yore," said Merlin, "that better is art than strength. Assemble your army to fetch them. I will go with it."

And then he sat still, as though he would from the world depart.

So Merlin sailed to Ireland with Uther and fifteen thousand knights. There Merlin led Uther, with a thousand of the knights (the rest remaining behind to guard the ships) "to where the Giants' Ring stood on the summit of a mountain, lifted high against the welkin. The thousand knights went all about, and earnestly beheld it. There stood the marvellous work, great and most strong.

Then said Merlin:

"Knights you are strong. Choose one of these stones; wreath it fast with sail-ropes; heave it with mighty tree-trunks."

They chose a stone. They wreathed it fast with sail-ropes. They heaved it with mighty tree-trunks, but that stone they could not stir.

Then Merlin said to Uther:

"Uther, draw back your knights as far as a man might cast a stone. Stand together, and let no man stir until you hear me cry. Take each of you a stone."

Uther drew back his knights. All stood and did not stir, beholding Merlin go about the stones. Thrice he went about them, thrice within and thrice without. His lips moved without ceasing, as though he were singing his beads.

Then he called aloud:

"Knights, take each of you a stone!"

Then came the knights into the Giants' Ring. Each laid
his arms about a giant stone. It heaved within them,
light as a feather ball.

They brought them to the ships. They sailed away from
Ireland. They beached on their own sea-strand. They
bore the stones to Ambresbury. There Merlin ranged
them in due order, as they had stood before.

"Then King Aurelie came, and made a great feast on
the plain. And all his merry folk came, blithe in breast
at this great wonder. On the third day the king had the
Ring hallowed. In English its name is Stonehenge."

Modern archaeology informs us:

"The source of the inner circle of the Stonehenge stones
is the Presely Hills in Wales, where, in Ordovician
times, volcanic activity forced up igneous rocks (known
as dolerite intrusions) from far below. The identity of
four Types of stones from that area with those compris-
ing the inner circle of Stonehenge was established between 1920 and 1923; they are believed to have been
erected there by the Beaker Folk about 1500 B.C. ... A
Bronze Age Road, which still leads into the Presely
Hills was established in that era by traffic which connected the centre of power of the Beaker Folk on Salis-
bury Plain with Whitesand bay, and from there by boat
with the copper and gold of the Wicklow Hills."

The Presely Hills are rich in megalithic monuments
connected with the Arthurian stories, such as the Bronze
Age *Bedd Arthur* (The Grave of Arthur); the Neolithic
Bedd-yr-Afanc (The Grave of Avanc, the prehistoric
monster which, in Welsh mythology, brought about the
Flood); the New Stone Age *Cerrig Meibion Arthur* (The

Stones of the Sons of Arthur), connected by hoary tradition with the Twich Trwyth, the boar who, in one of the Welsh *Mabinogion*, swims across the River Severn and is hunted across Devon.

Stonehenge is 135 miles from the Presely Hills. The transportation of its inner circle stones, weighing up to four tons each, would have been impossible by unaided prehistoric sledge and boat – would indeed, be beyond even our own modern technology.

But there are many stories of sonic engineering feats in ancient times. At the Fall of Jericho, for example, Joshua's army marched round the city (1,250 feet square, circumference about a mile), encompassing it once a day for six days, the priests blowing their long ram's horn trumpets.

"But on the seventh day they compassed the city seven times. And the seventh time, when the priests blew with the trumpets, Joshua said to the people, *Shout*. And the people shouted with a great shout. And the wall of the city fell down flat."

Can we not glimpse a certain delicate correspondence in Merlin's "going about the stones?" "Thrice he went about them, thrice within and thrice without. His lips moved without ceasing, as though he were singing his beads." And when each knight laid his arms about a giant stone, it heaved within them, light as a feather ball.

Layamon's simile is arresting. All true images are born of Imaginations. Merlin's sonic magic has literally given the massive boulders wings.

Out of his raising of the Giant's Ring near "Ambres-

bury", we recognise Merlin for what he really is. For
Stonehenge is the greatest of our English Druid Circles.
In Merlin we can see an Initiate of the Druidic Mys-
teries – an Initiate steeped in their pre-Christian lore,
yet, like them, aware of the descent of the King of the
Elements of the Earth.

Neither Wace nor Layamon gives a reason for Merlin's
fathering. But Sire Robert de Borron begins his *Joseph*
with God's sending of His Son to save mankind from
the power of the fallen spirits, following this with a picture, in his *Merlin*, of the wrath of these spirits and their
decision to make a counter-move. Infuriated by the
Decent of Christ into Hell, they plot the birth of a child
born of a human mother but fathered by a fiend.

The plot fails, for the mother is a nun, whose purity and
piety bar her child's inheritance of his father's will to
evil, but what he does inherit from him is his supersensible knowledge, and this he places at the service of
mankind.

De Borron describes Merlin as being born with a hairy
body. In Rudolf Steiner's lectures on the Gilgamesh
Epic, he mentions that Eabani (Enkidu), the wise counsellor of Gilgamesh, has such a body, and that this is to
be taken as a picture of his close connection with the
spiritual worlds.

Immediately after his baptism (at which he receives his
name of Merlin), the child successfully defends his
mother, who has been sentenced to death for his birth.
(In another version it is her confessor who convinces
her judges of her innocence.)

While Merlin is less than two years old, he dictates the

story of Joseph, the history of the Grail, and the circumstances of his own birth, to Blaise, called by some Grail
writers Merlin's "master", who commits it all to
parchment. It is said elsewhere in Grail literature that
to read and understand aright what Blaise has written
at Merlin's dictation is to ensure the soul's salvation.
It is illuminating to re-read his mother's description in
Layamon of Merlin's father. "There came to me the
fairest thing that ever was born. ... This thing glistened of gold." She is loth to call him "evil-thing"; her
heart would have him rather "on God's behalf dight."
The gentle, marvelling characterisation leads us to
Lucifer.
It holds for us the seed of an understanding of Merlin.
His is the Druidic wisdom, pre-Christian, given by
Lucifer. But into the cup of that wisdom has been
poured the new content of Christ.
Rudolf Steiner tells us;
"The mutual fertilisation of these two evolutionary
streams (Christ's and Lucifer's) began at the moment
when the sacrificial blood of the Christ flowing from the
Cross was received into the vessel of the Holy Grail and
brought to the West from the East ... Christ will give
the substance, Lucifer the form."

A kind of etheric geography governed the choice of the
sites of Druid Circles; where the veil was thin between
the spiritual world and the earthly, they could bring
down the wisdom of the one to guide and inform the
other.
But, given this primal relationship, other conditions
could also be auspicious. Rudolf Steiner speaks of how

the young Northern peoples brought into Christian culture the sight of the dead working on, and of how, "out
of the dissolving ether-bodies of the dead, something is
always preserved, so that we are surrounded by them."
Because ancient cromlechs and similar megalithic
centres of worship have often been found to be raised
over burial places (an example is the covered burial
places of Celtic heroes in Ireland), it has wrongly been
assumed that the bodies buried there were human sacrifices. But it was rather that the sites were specially
favourable because they were *already* burial places –
that here the dead could specially help and bless the
living.

Avalon was the most famous of such sacred burial-
places, with standing-stones erected over them to aid the
spiritual leaders of the people in their converse with the
cosmos. "The Isle of Avalon," wrote Maelgwyn, the
British bard, "hungry for burial, was once crowned,
more than all others in the world, by oracular circles of
prophecy." To the Druids Avalon, at the centre of its
mighty Star Temple, ten miles in diameter, written into
the Earth, was the first in spiritual power among "the
three mighty works of Britain." Stonehenge was the
second.

Layamon speaks of Hengist's love-day taking place in
a pleasant plain beside the Abbey of "Ambresbury."
There was indeed in Layamon's day such an Abbey
there – that Abbey of "Almesbury" in which, in Malory, Queen Guenever takes refuge after Arthur's
"death", and where she greets Sir Launcelot with the
woeful words, "Through thee and me is the flower of
kings and knights destroyed." But this Abbey stood on
the site of an earlier Druid College, in which, as in the
Druid Colleges of Chartres and Mona, the period of

initiation lasted twenty years.

In the light of all this we marvel at the quiet skill with which Wace and Layamon place before us the two inwardly connected pictures of Hengist's massacre of the Britons and Merlin's raising of the Giant's Ring above their burial-place.

With equally artless artistry they lead us, in a series of vivid pictures, through the preparation for and through the unfolding of Arthur's destiny, and Merlin's part in this.

Vortigern dies, and his outlaw son, Pascent, raises an army against King Aurelie, who lies sick at Winchester. "Uther led his brother's army against them in his stead. With Uther went Merlin."

Pascent sends "a heathen Saxon", Appas, to Winchester, to murder Aurelie. "Appas shaved his crown, and put on a hair shirt and a monk's black cowl and gown, and took herbs and poisons, and came to Winchester, and gave out that he was a leech sent by Uther, the king's brother. They brought him to the king's bedchamber, and he gave him a potion laced with scamony, a poison, and laid the king down.

"Then he said to the king's attendants:

"'Wrap the king well, that he may sweat out his sickness. Let him sleep till midnight'".

When they softly wakened him at midnight, the king whispered:

"I am swollen with poison. Soon I shall be dead. Let me lie at the east end of Stonehenge, and let Uther be king in my stead."

"So he drifted into death."

That night, above Uther's army in Wales, the moon
shone like a sun, "and a star appeared that cast forth a
terrible beam with a dragon's head at the end thereof,
and from its head came two bright beams.

'Merlin,' said Uther, 'rede me this token. For the sight
of it brings sorrow to my heart.'

"Merlin sate him still a long time, as if he with dream
fully greatly laboured. They said who saw it that oft he
turned as if he were a serpent. Then 'gan he to wake,
then 'gan he to quake.

"'Alas, he said, 'dead is Aurelie, noblest of kings. Now
are you lord of his lands and his men. You are that
dragon's head, and the two rays that come from its
mouth betoken a powerful son and a beloved daughter.
Now weapon your men and march forth to fight Pascent
before back we must ride.'

"And Merlin 'gan slumber as if he would sleep."

Uther slew Pascent in battle and, victorious, came to
Winchester, buried his brother Aurelie within
Stonehenge, and was made king. "In memory of the
comet, he caused two dragon's heads to be made, one to
remain in Winchester, and one to be borne before him
in battle. And therefore was the name laid on him of
Uther Pendragon."

Aided and advised by Gorlais, Earl of Cornwall, "a valiant knight, though stricken in years," Uther now won a
crushing victory over the Saxons – "he slew the heathen
in the wealds, slew over the fields the yellow locks." At
the feast given to celebrate this great victory , Gorlais
was given the place of honour opposite the king, and
next to him sat his wife, Ygaerne the Fair. This was the
first time Uther had seen Ygaerne, and he fell so shame-
lessly in love with her that the outraged Gorlais took
her home forthwith to his castle of "Tintaieol"

(Tintagel). "In this tower he sealed her close, leaving loyal thanes to guard her, while he, with the rest of his men-at-arms garnished, took refuge in his other strong keep. "Thither came Uther and his host, and for seven nights sat down before the tower, till his heart, dwelling ever on Ygaerne, was weary beyond measure of Gorlais and his castle."

At last he said to Ulfin, a thane grown old in wisdom:

"Ulfin, counsel me. For I may not have my will in any thing in this world's-realm."

"Sire,' said Ulfin, "you go a strange way to win a loyal lady's heart by harassing her lord. Some other way you must devise if you would win her."

"If Merlin were but with us on the host," said Uther, "he would tell me what to do to win to my desire. Ulfin, fair friend, fetch me Merlin."

Merlin is found in a wilderness, "standing beneath a tree." His greeting underlines the ebbing of spiritual knowledge between the twelfth century and the fifteenth.

For Malory, writing in the latter, sees this affair as a mere liaison; and the only hint of a mission necessary to evolution being involved is the condition on which Malory's Merlin consents to help Uther:

"'Sir, if you will be sworn to me, as ye be a true king anointed, to fulfil *my* desire, ye shall have *your* desire.'

"Then the king was sworn upon the Four Evangelists.

"'Sir,' said Merlin, 'this is my desire: the first night that ye shall lie beside Igraine, ye shall get a child on her; and when that is born, that it shall be delivered to me to nourish. For it shall be to your worship and to the child's avail.'

"'I will well,' said the king, 'as thou wilt have it.' …

"And when the lady was delivered, the king commanded two knight and two ladies to take the child, bound in a cloth of gold, and that ye deliver him to what poorman ye meet at the postern gate of the castle. "So the child was delivered unto Merlin, and so he bare it forth to Sir Ector, a passing true man and a faithful. And Merlin made an holy man to christen the child and named him Arthur. And Sir Ector's wife nourished the child with her own pap."

But in Layamon's twelfth century Chronicle, Merlin greets Uther's messenger thus:

"Friend, I know all. Uther seeks me, that I may come to him. True it is that without my aid he could never win Ygaerne. And true it is that win her he must; for to these two is to be born (though to neither is this known) a son who will not die as long as eternity lasts. As long as this world endures shall his glory stand."

Churchman though Layamon was, it would seem that he still retained some intimations of the workings of the Mysteries. Like the coming together of Lancelot and Elaine that Galahad might be born, Arthur's conception would seem to have been arranged by the Mysteries, with Merlin as hierophant. In it one can perhaps see a faint, imperfect foreshadowing of that eugenic occultism of the future of which Rudolf Steiner speaks. When Merlin makes his way from his tree in the wilderness to the hosts before the castle, he promises Uther:

"Sire, your will you shall have. I will make you so like Gorlais that Ygaerne and all her household will know you for no other. And Ulfin likewise shall be Jordan, the Earl's chamber-thane, and I myself his steward, Britael."

"Forth those three went, and so came to Tintaieol. At the castle-gate they called out, and the gate was lifted, and the guards met them with joy. The tidings went on wings to Ygaerne, and she on wings came to greet her lord. And that night was conceived their son Arthur."

On Ygaerne's part, therefore, the conception of Arthur was innocent.

Of the death of Gorlais, which made it possible for Uther to marry Ygaerne, Uther in turn was innocent. Layamon tells us in one of his vivid and strangely moving pictures:

"Now at daybreak it became known to Uther's thanes that the king was not among them. Lest alarm should spread through the host, and lest Gorlais should learn of this absence and sally forth to the attack, they thought it better themselves to be the attackers. So the trumpeters blew; and the men-at-arms assembled; and Cador the Standard-Bearer heaved the Dragon high; and Earl Aldoft of Gloucester, who had fought his way out of Hengist's love-day slaughter with a stake, took Uther's place; and so they marched against Gorlais' second castle.

"Out sallied Gorlais and his men; swiftly they fell and their lord with them; swiftly the castle was taken … As Uther and Ulfin and Merlin came back to their own host, they came each in his own shape. Joy filled the folk at their coming."

Again with an artist's hand Layamon spins a thread between the past and future. It is the ancient Earl Aldoft, the heroic survivor of Hengist's love-day, who, in taking Uther's place at the head of the army, makes it possible for the king to marry Ygaerne with hands guiltless of Gorlais' death.

"As soon as might be, Uther made Ygaerne his queen. In due time, Arthur was born, and after him Anna. Arthur was sent to Amorica, to be trained in kingship.

Uther ruled wisely, and had much love for his folk.
There was peace in the land."
Then the Saxons poisoned the well from which Uther
drank." A chamber-thane filled a golden bowl thereat
and bore the water to Uther. When he had drunk, his
heart burst."
Uther was buried within Stonehenge, beside his brother
Aurelie and all those kinsmen who had been slain at
Hengist's love-day; and the Briton sent for Arthur to
come home from Armorica and be made King.
The *Brut* and the *Roman de Brut* tell much of Arthur and
his many battles. But little do they tell us of the guidance
and the help he had from Merlin. To hear of these we
have to turn to the later Romances.
But Layamon would seem to have had a visionary
glimpse of Arthur as the mighty helper of successive
races on the island, for he ends his *Brut* upon this note;
"The *Britons* believe yet that Arthur is alive and dwelleth
in Avalon with the fairest of all elves, and the *Britons* ever
yet expect when Arthur shall return. Was never the man
born, or ever any lady chosen, who knoweth of the truth,
to say more of Arthur. But whilom was a sage high
Merlin; he said with words – his sayings were true – that
an Arthur should yet come to help the *English*."

REFERENCES

Wace, *Roman de Brut.*
Layamon, *Brut.*
The Presely Hills, Pembrokeshire Nat. Park Publication.
Joshua, Chapter VI,11-20.
Malory, *Morte d'Arthur.*

LECTURES by RUDOLF STEINER:

Prophecy, its Nature and Meaning,
  Berlin, 9th Nov. 1911.

The Mystery of the Trinity,
  23-30 July 1922. (Anthroposophic Press).

Esoteric Christianity,
  Neuchatel, 28 Sep. 1911. (R. Steiner Press).

The East in the Light of the West,
  Munich, 23-31 Aug. 1909.

CHAPTER XI

MERLIN IN MALORY AND THE DIDOT PERCEVAL

Prophecies." says Rudolf Steiner, "may or may not be accurate in every detail. What matters is that impulses connected with evolution as it moves on towards the future shall work upon and waken slumbering powers in man. In the striving for consciousness of the future a seed has formed as fire for our will."

"In Malory we find Merlin using his powers of prophecy to prepare the young King Arthur for such a new impulse connected with evolution – the approaching coming of the Grail to Britain. Intertwined with this prophecy is the intimation of Merlin's own approaching withdrawal from "this world's-realm." We are reminded of John the Baptist's "I must decrease that He may increase."

It is when, in Arthur's war with Nero, twelve kings on the enemy's side are killed in the same battle, that Merlin begins to prepare the young king for the coming of the Grail:

"All the twelve kings were buried in the church of St. Stephen's in Camelot; and King Arthur let make twelve images of laton and copper, over-gilt with gold, in the sign of the twelve kings; and each one of them held a taper of wax that burnt day and night; and King Arthur was made in sign of a figure standing above them with a sword drawn in his hand; and all the twelve figures had countenances like unto men who were overcome.

"All this Merlin made by his subtle crafts, and there he told the king:

"'When I am dead, these tapers shall burn no longer, and soon after shall the adventures of the Sangreal come among you and be achieved.'"

When peace was restored, the barons desired Arthur to marry. He consulted Merlin.

"Merlin asked him:

"'Is there any that ye love more than another?'

"'Yea,' said King Arthur. 'I love Guenever, the daughter of King Leodegrance of Cameliard. This damosel is to me the fairest and most valiant lady living.'

"'Sir,' said Merlin, 'an ye loved her not so well as ye do, I should find you another damosel.'

"And Merlin warned the king that Guenever was not wholesome for him to take to wife, for that Lancelot should love her and she him again. And he turned his tale to the adventures of the Sangreal."

Here Malory shows us clearly how freewill is fraught with fetters; if Arthur makes a certain decision, tragic consequences *must* follow. Merlin lays before him what seems at first sight a strange choice between Guenever and the Grail.

In Celtic folk-lore Guenever is the daughter of Ogyrven the Giant. A Welsh folk-rhyme runs:

> "Guenever, Giant Ogyrven's daughter,
> naughty young, more naughty later."

The *Book of Taliesin* records that "Three muses rise out

of the cauldron of Ogyrven the Giant." The Celtic goddess Ceridwen is called the Ogyrven of Seeds. Taliesin
sings:"I have been gifted with genius from the Cauldron of Ceridwen;" and the Welsh bard, Llyarch ab
Llwelyn, tells us: "God the Ruler gives me a ray of
melodious song from the Cauldron of Ceridwen."
Ceridwen,the goddess of poetic creativeness, is also the
goddess of the innocent generative powers of Nature.
"In the Druid Mysteries." says Rudolf Steiner, "the
chaste innocence that sleeps in the flower-buds – this, it
was felt, must enter right into the soul of the pupils."
And again, "the pupils were told how the body would
become chaste and plant-like as a calyx which turns its
cup toward the love-lance of the sun. This ideal was
called the Holy Grail."
In Malory, Merlin prophecies that "there should be
three white bulls that should achieve the Sangreal, and
two should be maidens and the third should be chaste."
– a prophecy which came to pass in Galahad, Percival
and Bors. But in choosing the unchaste Guenever for
his wife, Arthur debars himself from the Grail-Quest.
When the entire Round Table, fired by Gawaine,
responds to Camelot's Whitsunday visitation of the
Grail by vowing to fare forth on a twelvemonth quest of
it, all the hundred and fifty knights of the fellowship,
coming forth from the service in the minster, "put on
their helmets and mounted upon their horses, and rode
through the streets of Camelot; and there was weeping
of the rich and of the poor. And the King turned away,
and might not speak for weeping.
Yet it was a result of Arthur's choice of Guenever as a
wife that the Round Table, which had formerly been in
the keeping of his father, Uther Pendragon, and had
then passed out of it, now came into Arthur's care. For

Uther had given the Round Table to King Leodegrance, the father of Guenever, who now sent it to Arthur as a marriage-gift, together with a hundred good knights. It was then that Merlin set up the Round Table at Camelot for the Arthurian stream of knighthood, already, in an archetypal gesture, prophesying the future uniting of the Arthur stream and the Grail stream, by reserving at the table one seat, The Siege Perilous, in which only Galahad, the Arthurian Grail-hero, might safely sit.

It is out of Merlin's gift of prophecy that his own actions spring. He intervenes when Sir Pellinore would have slain King Arthur, "for in him the hopes of Logres lies." But he also brings his holy arts to the healing of the frustrated knight's condition – "he placed his hand on Sir Pellinore's head, and his battle-fury passed from him."

Merlin's prophetic powers, perceiving an action not yet performed, perceives also how its consequences beget further consequences which become the formative forces of the future. Thus he says to Sir Balyn:

"You shall strike the Dolorous Stroke; yet for the healing of that stroke shall the Holy Grail come to Logres, and the good knight Sir Galahad shall achieve it. Thereafter shall the darkness fall once more upon Logres.'

And now Merlin himself falls in love – with Nimue, "a damosel of the lake", who will be with the three queens veiled in black in the solemn barge which will one day come to take the wounded Arthur to Avalon. At the same time he tells Arthur that he, Merlin, "should not dure long, but in spite of all his crafts, would be put quick (alive) into earth." adding:

"Then had ye lever (rather) than all your lands to have me back again."

King Arthur not unreasonably replied:

"Since ye know of your adventures, put away that adventure by your crafts."

But Merlin knows that this is his fore-ordained destiny; he comprehends its meaning and accepts it. Already it has formed a seed of fire for his will.

"Nay, that may not be," he answers; and he departs from the king.

Malory, in every reference to Nimue except the one relating to Merlin, shows her as dedicated to cherishing and protecting Arthur and his fellowship; twice, indeed, she saved Arthur from the death devised for him by his sister, Morgan le Fay.

"Then came the Damosel of the Lake into the field, that put Merlin under the stone; for she knew how Morgan le Fay ordained that Arthur should have been slain that day, and therefore she came to save his life."

For Morgan le Fay had stolen Arthur's sword, the true Excalibur, and given it to his opponent, Sir Accolon, that he might slay Arthur with it; and Arthur, returning the knights blows with the false Excalibur, "found his sword bit not steel as it was wont to do. Then the Damosel of the Lake beheld Arthur, how full of prowess his body was, and the false treason that was wrought to him, for to have had him slain; and at the next stroke, by the Damosel's enchantment, the sword Excalibur, fell out of Accolon's hand to the earth.

"And therewithal Arthur lightly leapt to it, and gat it into his hand; and forthwithal he knew that it was his sword Excalibur, and said:

"'Thou hast been from me too long, and much damage hast thou done me.'"

So with the true Excalibur, Arthur conquers Accolon, and his own life (and Accolon's with it) is saved.

A second time Morgan le Fay plots against Arthur's life:

"Now there came a damosel from Morgan to the king, and she brought with her the richest mantle that ever was seen in that court.

"And the damsel said:

"'Your sister sendeth you this mantle, and desireth that you should take this gift of her.'

"And when the king beheld it, it pleased him much.

"Then came the Damosel of the Lake and said to him:

"'Sir, put not on you this mantle till ye have seen more, but command the bringer thereof to put it upon her.'"

When Arthur did so,she replied:

"Sir, it will not beseem me to wear a king's garment.'

But when Arthur insisted, "the garment was put upon her, and forthwithal she fell down dead and was burnt to coals."

And now Nimue comes to the aid of Sir Pelleas, whom the lady Ettard, whom he loves, has sworn to murder. Nimue enchants Sir Pelleas out of his woeful love for his would-be murderess, and into love with herself. "And the Damosel of the Lake rejoiced Sir Pelleas, and they loved together during their life's days."

Nimue appears again at King Arthur's Court to assure him of Queen Guinever's innocence of the death of Sir Patrise, "for ever she (Nimue) did great goodness to King Arthur and his knights through her sorcery and enchantments." Through these Nimue knew the truth of Sir Patrise's death, which was that "Sir Pinel le Savage had empoisoned apples to have slain Sir Gawaine, and by misfortune Sir Patrise ate one of those apples, and then suddenly he brast." The Queen was therefore acquitted, and the truth written upon the dead knight's tomb.

And, lastly, in the barge which came for Arthur, "also was there Nimue, the chief Lady of the Lake, that had wedded Pelleas the good knight; this lady had done much for King Arthur; and never would she suffer Sir Pelleas to be in no place in danger of his life, and so he lived to the uttermost of his days with her in great rest." At first sight it is not easy to reconcile the Nimue of these vignettes by Malory with the account, also by Malory, of her dealings with Merlin:

"Now it fell so that Merlin fell in a dotage on one of the damosels of the lake, high Nimue; he would let her have no rest, but would always be with her; and ever   she made him good cheer till she learned of him all manner of things that she desired. And Merlin went with her evermore wheresomever she went. Merlin showed her many wonders by the way; and so they came into Cornwall. And she was afeared of him because he was a devil's son.

"And so on a time Merlin showed to her a rock wherein was a great wonder, and wrought by enchantment, that went under a great stone. So by her subtle working she made Merlin to go under that stone to let her wit of the marvels there; but she wrought so there for him that he came never out for all the craft he could do. And so she departed and left Merlin."

Outside Malory we find other variants of this story. In these Nimue is called Viviane.

In one, set in the forest of Arvantes, Merlin has con- structed a tomb for himself. Viviane wishes to see if there would be room for them both in it. Having persuaded him to lie down in it, she closes the lid, which cannot be opened from within. So, like Nimue, Viviane is left free, and Merlin, "quick", for all the craft that he can do, is left imprisoned.

A Breton version, full of vivid and enlightening detail, sets the scene in the Forest of Broceliande, where Merlin comes upon Viviane beside the Fountain of Baranton (Sir Kynon's Fountain in the *Mabinogian*), coming to her "in the guise of a merry youth, drawing near by many treacherous pathways barred by thorns and green boughs."

As their love ripened, "Viviane cast about how she could detain him for evermore.

"'Sir, I would have you teach and show me how to enclose and imprison a man, without a tower, without walls, without chains, but by enchantment alone, in such manner he may never be able to go out, except by me.'

"'Certes, lady, yes. Tell me what you would have.'

"'Sir, I would that we should make a fair place and a suitable, so contrived by art and by cunning that it might never be undone, and that you and I should be there in joy and in solace.'

"'My lady, all this will I perform.'

"'Sir, I would not have *you* do it; but you shall teach *me*, and *I* will do it. Then it will be more to my will.'

"'I grant you this.'

"Then Merlin began to devise, and the damsel put it all in writing. And when he had devised the whole, then had the damsel full great joy.

"And as they were going one day, hand in hand, through the Forest of Broceliande, they found a bush of whitethorn which was laden with flowers. And they seated themselves upon the green grass under the shade of this whitethorn, and Merlin laid his head upon the damsel's lap and fell asleep.

"Then Viviane rose and made a ring with her wimple round the bush and round Merlin; and she began her enchantments, such as he himself had taught her.

"Nine times she made the ring; and nine times she made the enchantments. And then she went and sat by him, and placed his head again upon her lap.

"When Merlin woke and looked about him, it seemed to him that he was enclosed in the strongest tower in the world, and laid upon a fair bed.

"'My lady, unless you will abide with me you have deceived me; for to unmake this tower no-one on earth hath power.'

"And Merlin never went out of that tower wherein Viviene had enclosed him. But she entered and went out again whenever she so listed."

Some of the other Arthurian cycles portray Nimue-Viviane in a different light. In these Merlin accepts, out of his initiate-knowledge, that "all things work by the will of God;" and he sees what Malory portrays as heartless imprisonment as the next stage of the journey of that part of man which knows no death – as when he speaks of Nimue as "the damsel who is to call me to my long sleep."

Indeed, in the Middle English prose romance, *Merlin*, Nimue already plainly indicates that interpretation to which we ourselves are guided by meditative musing – "I give you rest, that you may sleep through many centuries till the day dawns for you to wake."

And our earlier picture of Nimue as helper of Arthur emerges enhanced in her explanation to Merlin of why she herself may not stay with him under the stone:

"Needs must I go forth again, for King Arthur is in dire

danger; and sith that you may no longer counsel him, it is I who must now give him aid."

This could, in fact, give new meaning and dimension to Nimue's eager learning of all the holy magical arts that Merlin can teach her. In this context we can even see her as taking over part of Merlin's karma.

Not until our own times has the folk-belief died that the whitethorn is the abode of fairies. It was a folk-belief based on supersensible knowledge; for where a whitethorn grows, the etheric forces are strong. When Viviane weaves an enchanted tower about him with her wimple, Merlin awakes in the etheric world. The "marvels" which Merlin finds under the stone" in Malory are also not of the physical plane, and it is with his own consent and foreknowledge of what the result will be that he enters to explore them. When Nimue "puts Merlin under the stone", it is clear that the early Arthurian writers did not regard this as a hostile incarceration, however much of this fact may have been obscured by the change of consciousness in Malory's time, for the early illuminations show Nimue and Merlin lying peacefully together within the rock, listening to harpers playing on bright red harps.

This scene is, in fact, so vividly reminiscent of illuminations of Tristan and Isolt in their Minnegrotto that one wonders whether there may not have been some arcane significance now forgotten in archaic remains such as Orkney's Hoy Stone (thirty-six feet long, eighteen feet broad, nine feet deep), which an archaeologist of last century described as follows:

"No other stones are near it. 'Tis all hollowed within by

human art, having a door at the east end two foot square, with a stone of the same dimension lying about two feet from it, intended, no doubt, to close the entrance. Where there is, at the south end of it, cut out, the form of a bed and pillow capable to hold two persons." The troubadour Gottfried von Strassburg, who tells us in the prologue to his *Tristan and Isolt* that it is "for the delights of lofty spirits" that he writes, describes how, alone together in the wilderness, in their Minnegrotto, with its crystalline bed, "they looked at one another, and on that they lived. That which grew in the eyes of each was food. There they had no food but that of the spirit and love."

The word "crystalline" enlightens us as to the true natures of Merlin's rock.

"Entering the crystal" was the description given in earlier times to a certain state of consciousness, when a man went forth from his body in full awareness and was able to behold the supersensible worlds and to feel united with the deeds of supersensible beings. This, as we have seen, was a spiritual activity which in the Druids had come to a special flowering. There were places where this activity was aided by the thinness of the veil between the material and the non-material; at such places the Druids established their Mystery Centres (and, later, the Celtic monks their Christian churches and monastic schools).

A variant of the story of Merlin and Viviane describes how she wove with her wimple not an invisible tower but a house of glass. Because of its transparency, glass conveyed the same meaning. Avalon, that entrance to supersensible worlds, is referred to as the Isle of Glass – in the Latin of the chroniclers as *Insula Vitrea*; in the Celtic of the bards as *Ynesguitrin*; in the Old French of the Grail-cycles as *Ile de Voirre*.

It is with wonder and awe that one discovers that, in Icelandic, *vitrin* means "a revelation, as in great wisdom or a vision," and *vitringer* means "a wise man, an Initiate." For now one can appreciate with what spiritual exactitude the transparency of the soul emerging into the invisibility of the soul-realm as it moves through it in supersensible form is imaged forth in the boat of glass by which Initiates travel to the Land of Heart's Desire. In the *Echtra Condla*, Condla, a Celtic prince of the second century A.D., travels thither in this way; and Merlin had a house of glass in which he sailed the seas of higher worlds. While in Taliesin's poem, *Preiddeu Annum*, in which Arthur sailed on an Initiation-voyage with twelve companions, we are told that "beyond the *Caer Wydr* (the Enclosure of Glass) they beheld not the prowess of Arthur."

The crystal which is thus entered is both heavenly and earthly. The former is the Crystal heaven, the realm of the fixed stars, which all men enter in sleep. Though only those on a path of spiritual development do so consciously. In *Preiddeu Annum*, it is to *Caer Sidi* (the Enclosure of the Zodiac) that Arthur sails first. The Star Temple spread round Glastonbury like a reflection of this Crystal Heaven thus holds before the eye of the soul the picture of Avalon as the Isle of Glass.

The other crystal which is entered is that of the crystal-line earth itself, formed by the substance poured out in sacrifice by those higher beings with whose deeds man is united in this higher consciousness. (In *Preiddeu Annum*, Arthur sails right from the Zodiac down into the bone-fortress of that most mineral part of man's body, the skeleton – the skeleton which Initiates in the Middle Ages saw in vision as already turned to crystal through Christ's Blood.) So we find Initiate-heroes who in life had reached this stage of consciousness being thought of as not dead but sleeping in crystal, awaiting their recall to new tasks on earth. It is in this sense that Malory writes of Arthur:

"Some men yet say, in many parts of England, that King Arthur is not dead, but had by the will of our Lord Jesu Christ gone into another place; and men say that he will come again, and he shall win the holy cross. I will not say that it shall be so, but rather I will say that here in this world he changed his life."

So it is to the Isle of Glass that Arthur is brought to be cured of his wound. Chrétien de Troyes, in his *Eric*, describes the *Ile de Voirre* as a happy land where there is no thunder or lightning, nor tempest, nor serpent, nor excessive heat or cold, blessed with eternal spring and with fruit and flowers growing without labour. We recognise from the description an Avallonian version of the Greeks' Elysium, of Keelta's Country of the Ever-Young, of Finn's Land of the Living Dead.

And since this realm we penetrate at night is also the realm of the so-called dead, we can understand how, through the Imaginations with which the air above the Tor was filled, the Isle of Glass acquired a special veneration "an island sacred to the dead, a place of rest for the spirits of the departed." Such Imaginations lingered longer in the ether over Druid Centres than elsewhere; and by the time St.Collen came to dwell at the foot of the Tor, he felt them to have outlived their period and purpose. And so we get this story:

Above the top of Glastonbury Tor hovered Caer Wydr, the Enclosure of Glass. The king of Caer Wydr invited St. Collen to visit him, and St. Collen climbed the Tor, armed with a flask of holy water. Overhead he saw a

wonderful castle of glass, filled with sweet music and
beautiful youths and maidens, all clad in blue and red.
"Blue is the colour of ice," replied St. Collen. "and red
is the colour of fire; and these man's soul must meet
with after death."
He sprinkled the holy water. The music ceased; the
king, the castle of glass, the beautiful youths and
maidens, all vanished into thin air; and St. Collen stood
alone on the top of the Tor.
It is a moving picture of the fading of the old clairvoyance.

Nimue-Viviane is the cherished pupil of a Druid. He has
endowed her richly with his own esoteric lore. She can
share with him, as Nimue, his "marvels beneath the
stone," or, as Viviane, "this fair place, where you and I
can be in joy and solace." Yet though she still inhabits
an earthly body, she can go in and out at will, for she
has Initiate knowledge. But Merlin never goes out, for
though he is "quick", he moves and breathes and has
his being in the supersensible world till the time is ripe
for him to incarnate in an earthly body again.

One version of Merlin's withdrawal from the Arthurian
scene is that he disappeared into his house of glass on
Bardsey Island, taking with him nine bards and the
Thirteen Treasures of Britain, and has never been seen
again. In the *Didot Perceval*, he survives Arthur, and he
brings the tidings of that last battle to Blaise, who
writes it all down and brings it to Perceval, who has

become Grail-King, and among the things he tells him is "how the Knights of the Round Table have completed their time."

There is no Merlin in Wolframs's *Parzival*; but in the story of this Grail hero as told in the *Didot Perceval*, Merlin's presence is felt throughout. He is referred to always as "the good enchanter" or "the wise enchanter"; his connection with Christianity is constantly stressed, as when he assures Arthur, "I will advise you towards nothing that may be contrary to the will of our Lord," or when he forewarns the King, "I may stay no longer in the world of men, for I have not my Saviour's permission."

In the same way in other cycles he speaks of his foreknowing "through my holy arts"; and in the *Mort Artu* even the bitter-tongued Keu (Kay) says of him to Arthur:

"You know well that Merlin is the wisest man in the world, and has never been taken in a lie."

In the *Didot Perceval*, The Round Table has not seats for a hundred and fifty knights, as in Malory, but thirteen; for it is modelled on the Table of the Last Supper. Of its installation at the Festival of Pentecost we are told:

"When mass had been sung, the King brought his twelve peers and seated them in twelve of the places; but the thirteenth signified the place where Judas sat, and Merlin kept it empty."

At the jousting at the Festival of Pentecost, the young Perceval li Gallois excelled so greatly in feats of arms that Arthur granted the boon he asked – that he might sit in this Siege Perilous.

"And as soon as he was seated, the stone split beneath him, with such an agonising sound that is seemed the Earth might sink into the abyss.

"'And a voice said:

"King Arthur, you have trespassed the commandment of which Merlin taught you. And this Perceval has wrought the rashest act that ever did any man. Know that thereof the Fisher-King has fallen into great infirmity and will never have cure, nor this stone be reunited, till he who will have the prize for chivalry in the whole world asks him what one does and whom one serves with the Grail.'"

Then the Knights of the Round Table rode out on the Grail Quest; and when they came to a cross where many ways met, they parted, and each took a separate path.

Perceval rode so far through the forest that he found many adventures, and presently came to "the castle where his father had lived, and his mother also; and now it remained to the damsel who was his sister."

She tells him of their mother's death from mourning for his absence, and brings him to a nearby hermitage to be blessed by the hermit, their uncle, who tells him:

"Your grandfather, the Fisher-King, cannot die till you have been to his court and have received the Grail into your keeping. Then you will be the guardian of the blood of Our Lord Jesu Christ."

Seeking the Fisher-King's castle, Perceval came to a beautiful tree beside a cross where four roads met. In it two children, all nude, about six years old were going from branch to branch. When he had watched them awhile, he called to them in the name of the Trinity:

"If ye be of God, speak to me."

And they replied:

"Know that we come from that paradise whence Adam was driven. You will take this way that lies to the right

hand before you to lead you to Brons, your grandfather."

Then they vanished from his sight, and "he considered
deeply in his heart, fearing they were only phantoms.

"Then from the midst of a great shadow a voice spoke:
"'Perceval, Merlin makes known to you that these children came from Jesu Christ our Saviour."

And Perceval, much comforted, rode to the castle of the
Fisher-King.

Here, as in Wolfram's *Parzival*, he forebore to ask the
healing question; here also, on his riding away from the
castle, a weeping maiden reveals to him the tragic consequences of silence.

The writer believed by some Arthurian scholars to be
De Borron, complaining of "other trouvères who
embroider their tales to make their ryhmes pleasant,"
confines himself to "only as much as Merlin has caused
to be written by Blayse, his master. For Merlin saw and
knew the adventures that happened to Perceval each
day, and he had them recorded by Blayse so that they
might be spoken of to worthy men who would wish to
hear them."

He tells us that for seven years Perceval wandered; and
at the end of them Merlin came to him, bearing a
scythe and clad in the form of the reaper.

"Know that I am called Merlin," he said. "Before you
were born your name was known to me."

"God witness, Merlin," said Perceval, "I have heard
much good spoken of you, and that you are a wise
prophet. In God's name, tell me how I shall find the
house of the rich Fisher-King."

So once more Merlin gave him wise guidance,
adding:

"Have a care when you come there that you ask about

whatsoever you see."

And this time, as "from the chamber there issued the lance that bled from its point, and after this the Grail and the damsel who bore the little platters of silver," Perceval does indeed ask the crucial question:

"Sire, tell me what one serves with these things that I see borne there."

"And as he spoke, he looked and saw that the Fisher King was changed in his nature, and was cured of his malady, and was as healthy as a fish."

Then Brons taught Perceval the sacred words which Christ had taught Joseph in prison, and which Joseph had in turn taught Brons, "which I cannot and ought not to tell you, and on the third day after this, David came with his harp and a host of angels with censers, and they bore the soul of Brons to heaven.

"And Perceval stayed there; and the enchantments disappeared throughout the world.

"And on this same day, King Arthur was at the Round Table that Merlin had founded, and they heard a crash of such greatness that they sat in fear. And the stone re-united that had split when Perceval sat in the empty place. And when Merlin came, they asked him concerning it."

And Merlin answered:

'Arthur, know that in your time is fulfilled a great prophecy. For the Fisher King is cured, and Perceval is Lord of the Grail, and Our Lord has given him in keeping His exalted blood to guard. And this is the reason that the stone is re-united that had split beneath him."

"Then Merlin took leave of Arthur, and bore Blayse with him to the dwelling of Perceval, the rich Fisher King, and there he stayed in the company of the Grail till Arthur had been taken by the three queens to Avalon, to be cured of his wounds."

The story ends on this strange note:
"Then Merlin came to Perceval and to Blaise; and he took leave of them and told them that Our Lord did not wish that he should show himself again, yet that he would not be able to die before the end of the world, but that then he would enjoy the eternal joy."
He continues:
"Now would I make a lodging outside your palace,and dwell therein, and prophecy whatever Our Lord commands me. And all those who see my lodging will name it the *esplumoir* of Merlin."
The manuscript ends:
"Then Merlin left them and made his *esplumoir*, and entered within; and never since then has he been seen in the world."
Arthurian scholarship has been much puzzled by Merlin's *esplumoir*. Even as late as 1960 an eminent authority comments:
"No entirely satisfactory explanation has ever been given as to what Merlin's *esplumoir* may have been."
In *Meraugis and Portlesguez*, a French verse-romance by Raoul de Houdenc, Merlin's *esplumoir* appears again. In this romance twelve prophetic maidens are sitting on the top of a high rock. Meraugis rides towards them and asks if they can direct him to Merlin's *esplumoir*. One of the maidens, pointing downwards at the rock on which they sit, replies, "Lo, here it is!"
Meraugis and Portlesguez applies the *Didot Perceval's* name to *Le Morte d'Arthur's* picture. Merlin's surely somewhat exposed lodging outside Perceval's palace has been replaced by Nimue's rock hidden deep in the forest.

In mediaeval French the verb *esplumer* meant "to pluck out feathers," and an *esplumer* was the cage in which birds were kept during the moulting season.[8] Does not the *esplumer* of Merlin suggest to the anthroposophist the picture of the soul, stripped of the physical garments ("feathers") of its past incarnation, withdrawn from earthly life till the time is ripe to put on the fresh feathers of a new one?

What Merlin's new incarnation was we already know from Rudolf Steiner. He tells us that Merlin came to earth again as Richard Wagner.

How livingly this indication deepens our understanding of this towering, complicated and perplexing personality!

In the light of Merlin's preparation in Arthurian times for the coming of the Grail, we bring a quickened understanding to Rudolf Steiner's statement that "Wagner's music purifies the ether-body."

Also, in the light of Merlin's stature as a Celtic Initiate, do we to Rudolf Steiner's further statement:

"Wagner possessed an unerring feeling for the world-situation and felt what tasks were incumbent upon the races. He felt it just as clearly as if he had known Spiritual Science."

And a glimpse of how the tasks of a later incarnation can be linked with, and even be a continuation of, an earlier one is given us in Dr. Steiner's words:

"We must think of Wagner as one who possesses deep knowledge and understanding, and whose desire it is to resuscitate for the people of modern times the Mysteries of the Holy Grail."

Musing on this, we remember how Rudolf Steiner has
told us that esoteric revelations and impulses and the
fruits of an earth-life's work may be laid up in the
spiritual atmosphere of the Earth by discarnate souls on
their way to supersensible worlds, and that these can be
gathered-in again by the same or by other souls on their
later journey down to Earth and here brought to further
fruition. Does not our own being say "yes" to the picture of this great soul committing the fruits of his
Merlin-incarnation to the cosmic ether at the close of
that earth-life, and as Wagner gathering them in, for
their re-birth, on his way down to the next?

REFERENCES

Prophecies of Merlin.
Légendes Traditionelles de la Bretagne.
Trace of the Elder Faiths in Ireland, Woodmartin,
Romance of Merlin.
History of the Druids, Tolland.
Notes to the Didot Perceval, Professor W. Roach.
Arthurian Literature in the Middle Ages, Professor
R.S. Loomis.
Ibid.

LECTURES by RUDOLF STEINER:

Richard Wagner in the Light of Anthroposophy,
  Berlin, 28 March and 19 May 1905. See NSL 175-8.

Parsifal,
  Berlin, 19May 1905, see NSL 175-8 and
  Landin/Mark 29 July 1906, in "The Christian
  Mystery" (Completion Press).

Richard Wagner and Mysticism,
  Berlin, 2 Dec. 1905.

CHAPTER XII

GALAHAD WORKETH ALL BY MIRACLE

W hen the newly knighted Galahad comes to King Arthur's Court, on that Day of Pentecost when the Grail also appears there,* he is clad all in red. Percivale, who feels a great drawing of the heart towards him, later asks that wise recluse, his aunt:

"Now, fair aunt, tell me what is the knight that bare the red arms on Whitsunday?"

And she replies:

"Wit ye well that otherwise he ought not to do than to go in red arms; and wit ye well that same knight hath no peer, for he worketh all by miracle, and he shall never be overcome of none earthly man's hand."

Galahad is only fifteen years old when he is knighted. Though this happened also with Sir Bors' son, Helayne le Blanc, it was not the normal procedure. The usual steps in the life of chivalry were:

To be made a page at the age of seven (i.e. at the birth of the etheric body);

To be made a squire at the age of fourteen (at the freeing of the astral body);

To be made a knight at twenty-one (at the drawing-in of the ego).

In Wolfram we have placed before us the Imagination

---

* See Study VI: *The Wandering Viaticum*

of the youthful Parzival's meeting with a Red Knight holding a golden goblet at the entrance to a castle. It is a picture of himself taking possession of his own body with the forces of puberty. In most men these forces acquire a certain guilt in that they enter the sphere of consciousness and become linked with the personal desire-nature.

That this was so to a certain degree even in Parzival is indicted by his musing on Condwiramur till Gawain breaks the spell by spreading a silken handkerchief over the drops of blood on the snow. Helayne's soubriquet of "le Blanc" suggests that in him these forces have remained innocent. That they have done so in Galahad to an enhanced degree is clear from the reiterated indications that he is "clene from sin." He should always bear red arms because in him the colour is redeemed from that of the desire-sullied blood to – as King Mordrains later says – the pure fire of the rose.

An aura of holy mystery surrounds Galahad when he comes to Camelot. He is brought by "a good man, and an ancient, clothed all in white, and there was no man knew from whence he came." This young knight, "so tender of age", gives the assembly gentle – one might almost say Rosicrucian – greeting: "Peace be with you, fair lords." He quietly takes the seat which bears his name at the Round Table – the Siege Perilous, "where there never sat none before but he was mischieved... And all the knights marvelled greatly of Sir Galahad, and wist not from whence he came but all only by God."

The empty scabbard hanging at his side was Balin's scabbard, left by Merlin for Galahad to find on an island reached by a bridge of iron and steel that was but half a foot broad. The sword which he drew from the stone afloat in the river was Balin's sword of the Dolorous Stroke, also placed there by Merlin for Galahad to find and so redeem it.

Galahad had come to Camelot without a shield.

"Sir," said the king, "a shield God shall send you."

But before this happened, Galahad had shown his miraculous mettle in the jousts in the meadows of Camelot without one.

"Then Sir Galahad, at the prayer of the King, did on his helm; but shield he would take none for no prayer of the King.

"Then Sir Galahad dressed him in the middest of the meadow, and there he began to break spears marvellously, so that all men had wonder of him. For he there surmounted and exceeded all the knights save twain, that were Sir Launcelot and Sir Percivale."

When the Arthurian knights set out on the Grail-Quest, "Galahad, as yet without shield, rideth alone," and comes to a White Abbey, where he finds another Knight of the Round Table, King Bagdemagus.

In Chrétien de Troyes' *The Knight of the Cart*, Bagdemagus is King of the Land of No Return, where he gives Queen Guinevere courteous and fatherly asylum when his evil son, Sir Meleagant, abducts her, and where his daughter, as good as her brother is evil, with self-sacrificing love seeks, finds and releases Lancelot from the terrible tower in which Meleagant has imprisoned him.

In the French prose romance, *Le Livre de Lancelot del Lac*, she again releases Lancelot from captivity – this time from the dungeon of Arthur's half-sister, the enchantress Morgan le Fay. Leading him safely from the castle through twelve locked doors, she provides him with horse, armour, spear and a plain white shield; and as the nameless Knight he fights nobly on her ageing father's behalf at a great tournament.

In this contrast of devilish son and angelic daughter, one can perhaps glimpse a dichotomy in King Bagdemagus which explains why he does not achieve the Grail even though Malory records that "he finds a branch of a holy herb that was the sign of the Sancgreal, and no Knight found such tokens but he was a good liver."

Though he chides Meleagant for his evil deeds, he does so indulgently and over-gently; and when Sir Tor is appointed to a seat at the Round Table in preference to himself, he departs from Camelot in wrath. Yet he is in some degree an initiate, for he is the knight (indeed, the only person) of whom Malory records that he conversed with Merlin after Nimue had "put him under the stone." He is on the path of striving; but there is still much in him awaiting transmutation.

At the White Abbey, King Bagdemagus explains to Galahad that he is here on an adventure – the Adventure of the White Shield. A monk shows it to them behind the altar, where "the shield hung as white as any snow, but in the middes was a red cross."

He warns King Bagdemagus:

"Sir, this shield ought not to be hanged about no knight's neck but he be the worthiest knight of the world."

"Well," says King Bagdemagus, "I wot well that I am not the best knight of the world, but yet I shall essay to bear it."

"And so he bare it out of the monastery," begging

Galahad to 'abide here till ye hear how I shall speed."
When King Bagdemagus and his squire had ridden two
miles, they were met, in a fair valley beside a hermitage,
by a knight in white armour riding a white horse. They
dressed their spears against each other, and the White
Knight struck so hard that he "brake the mails, and
thrust King Bagdemagus through the shoulder, and so
bare him from his horse."
He took the white shield saying:
"Knight, thou hast done thyself great folly, for this
shield ought not to be born but by him that shall have
no peer that liveth."
And to King Bagdemagus's squire he said:
"Bear this shield to the good knight Sir Galahad, that
ye left in the abbey, and greet him well from me."
"Sir," said the squire, "what is your name?"
"Take no heed of my name," said the knight, "for it is
not for thee to know, nor for none earthly man. But
know that this shield behoveth unto no man but unto
Sir Galahad.
When the squire brought the shield to Galahad, he
asked for his arms, and mounted his horse, and hung
the white shield about his neck, and came to where the
White Knight awaited him, "and every each saluted
other courteously."
"Sir," said Galahad, "by this shield be many marvels
fallen?"
And the White Knight told him, as Sarras, Joseph of
Arimathea made the white shield for his friend, King
Evelake, and how, when Joseph "was laid in his deadly
bed", his friend begged:
"Leave me some token of yours that I may think on
you."
Then there, upon that shield, Joseph made a cross of his

own blood. And he said:

"It shall always be as fresh as it is now, unto the time that Galahad, the good knight, the last of my lineage, shall bear it about his neck, and shall do marvellous deeds."

And when he had said this, the White Knight vanished away.

When Galahad returned to the White Abbey, he was received with joy. As he alighted from his horse, a monk came and begged him to go with him to a tomb in the churchyard. Such noises came from it that "who that heard should verily nigh be mad or lose his strength."

"Sir," he added, "we deem it is a fiend."

"Lead me thither," said Galahad; and all armed save his helm he followed him.

As they drew near to the tomb, a voice from within cried piteously:

"Sir Galahad, servant of Jesu Christ, come though not nigh, nor make me go again where I have been so long."

Galahad lifted the stone lid of the tomb; "and there came out a foul smoke; and after it he saw the foulest figure leap out that ever he saw in the likeness of a man."

And Galahad blessed him:

Then he heard a voice say:

"Galahad, I see there environ about thee so many angels that my power may not dare thee."

And then a good man came to him and said:

"Sir, I shall tell you what betokeneth all that you saw in the tomb. For that covered body betokeneth the duress of the world and the great sin that Our Lord found in the world."

And Galahad answered:

"Truly, I believe you right well.'

Once it happened that Galahad had not heard mass as he was wont to do before departing from any castle. So, coming to a deserted chapel on a mountain, "he entered and kneeled before the altar and besought God of wholesome counsel. And as he prayed, he heard a voice that said:

"'Go thou now to the castle of maidens, and there do thou away the evil customs.'"

Galahad, riding on, came to "a strong castle with deep ditches beside a fair river high Severn." Seven knights rode out of the castle, "and they were all brethren." Together they attacked him.

Galahad "smote the foremost to the earth, and with great force made them to forsake the field." The keys of the castle were brought to him, and a horn of ivory, "bounden with gold richly." With this Galahad called together all the knights who held their lands of the castle, "and made them do homage and fealty to the king's daughter the seven knights had held in bondage in the castle, and set them in great ease of heart."

The following day the seven brothers were encountered and slain by Gawaine, Gareth and Uwaine. Gawaine was told by the holy man in whose hermitage he spent the night:

"The seven knights ye slew betoken the seven deadly sins. Sir Galahad beat them all seven the day before; but his living is such, he shall slay no man lightly. As the Son of the High Father brought all the souls that were in prison out of thrall, so did Sir Galahad deliver all the maidens out of the woeful castle."

And now Sir Galahad fares with Percivale's sister to the Ship of Solomon, where, with Percivale and Bors, he receives her esoteric instruction;* with these three, in the Waste Forest, he shares the mystical experience of the white hart led by four lions;** with these three he comes to the castle where Percivale's sister freely sacrifices her own life for another's.*

"Now," said Percivale unto Galahad, "we must depart, so pray we our Lord we may meet together in short time."

During that short time, Galahad and Lancelot met and dwelt together for half a year in the ship in which the body of Percivale's sister lay. They had many adventures together; "but those adventures were with the wild beasts and not in the Quest of the Sancgreal, therefore the tale maketh here no mention thereof."

Then, arriving near a cross at the edge of a forest, "they saw a Knight armed all in white, that led in his right hand a white horse. He came to the ship, and saluted them, and said:

"Galahad, sir, ye have been long enough with your father. Come out of the ship, and start upon this horse, and go where the adventures shall lead thee in the Quest of the Sancgreal."

And, having "kissed his father sweetly," Galahad did so.

* See Study V: *Percivale's Sister and the Ship of Solomon*

** See Study I: *The Woodward of Broceliande*

Percivale, when he left his aunt the recluse with her
prophecy, "Galahad worketh all by miracle", ringing in
his heart, had heard mass in a monastery in which,
"behind the altar, he saw a rich bed and a fair, as of
cloth of silk and gold." On it lay "a passing old man,
and he seemed to be of the age of three hundred
winter." He wore a crown of gold, and his body was full
of great wounds.

"And ever he held up his hands over Our Lord's body
and cried:

"Fair sweet father, Jesu Christ, forget me not. Fair
Lord, let me never die till the good knight of my blood
of the ninth degree be come, that I may see him openly,
that he shall achieve the Sancgreal, that I may kiss
him."

And now that good knight of his blood has come. When
Galahad comes to the abbey, and, like Percivale, hears
mass there, King Mordrains' blind eyes see him. And
he cries out:

"Galahad, servant of Christ, Whose coming I have abi-
den so long, embrace me and let me rest on thy breast.
For thou art above all knights as the flower of the lily;
and thou art the rose, the flower of all good virtues, and
in the colour of fire. For the fire of the Holy Ghost is
taken so in thee that my flesh, which was of dead oldness, is made young again."

Galahad embraced him.

Then said the ancient king:

"Fair Lord Jesu Christ, now I have my will. Come
Thou and visit me."

And his soul departed from his body.

Then Galahad "put him in the earth as a king ought to be."

Departing, Galahad came into "a perilous forest," where he found a well which boiled with great waves. He put his hand into it, and the boiling ceased and the heat departed.

Thereafter it was known as Galahad's Well, " for that it brent, it was a sign of lechery, the which was that time much used; but that heat might not abide his pure virginity."

In the country of Gore he came to an Abbey founded by Joseph of Arimathea's son, and in this he found the tomb of King Bagdemagus. In a croft under the minster he also saw a tomb "which burned full marvellously." At his desire, the brethren led him down "gretys" (steps) into the cave; and at his coming "the flaming failed and the fire staunched."

A voice cried from the tomb:

"God hath given you a good hour, that ye may draw out the souls into the joys of Paradise. I am of your kindred, and have dwelt in this heat three hundred four and fifty winters, to be purged of the sin that I did against Joseph of Arimathie."

Then Galahad took in his arms the body in the tomb, and bore it up the stairs into the minster. And next morning, when mass had been sung, he laid it in the earth before the high altar.

And now "the three white bulls"are drawn together
again at Carbonek, where the Grail makes its last and
most solemn appearance in Logres*. The three board
their ship, whither the Grail has preceded them, and sail
to Sarras, where the body of Percivale's sister awaits
them, and "they bury her as richly as a King's daughter
ought to be."

The King of Sarras puts them in prison, where – like
Joseph of Arimathea – they are fed by the Grail. At the
death of the King, a voice bids the city choose the
youngest of the three knights in his place. So "by all the
assent of the holy city," Sir Galahad becomes king.

When Galahad has "borne the crown of gold" for the
space of a year, early one morning the three knights see
"a man in the likeness of a bishop" kneeling before the
Grail,"and about him a great fellowship of angels."

"And when he came to the consecrating of the the mass,
and had done, he called Sir Galahad and said to him:

"'Come forth, servant of Jesu Christ, and thou shalt see
that which thou hast much desired to see.'"

"And then Sir Galahad began to tremble right sore when
the deadly flesh began to behold the spiritual things.
And he held both his hands towards heaven and said:

"'Now, blessed Lord, I would no longer live, if it might
please thee.'

"Therewith the good man took our Lord's body between
his hands, and proffered it to Sir Galahad; and he
received it right gladly and meekly.

"'Wottest thou whom I am?" said the good man. "I am

* See Study VI: *The Wandering Viaticum*

Joseph of Arimathea, whom our Lord hath sent here to thee to bear thee fellowship.'

"Then Sir Galahad went to Sir Percivale and kissed him, and knelt down before the table and made his prayers; and a great multitude of angels bore his soul up to heaven. And his two fellows saw come from heaven a hand that came to the vessel and took it, and the spear, and so bore them up to heaven.

"Since then there was never no man so hardy for to say that he had seen the Sancgreal."

Sir Percivale and Sir Bors buried Galahad beside Percivale's sister. Then Percivale entered a hermitage as a religious; "and Bors was always with him, but never changed his secular clothing because he purposed him to go again into the realm of Logres."

When Percivale died, Bors buried him beside his sister and Galahad, then "entered a ship," which brought him straight to Camelot.

And here Sir Lancelot took him in his arms and said:

"Wit ye well, gentle cousin, that you and I will never depart in sunder whilst that our lives may last."

"Sir," said Sir Bors, "I will as ye will."

If we pay attention to the succession of incidents in which Galahad plays a part, we find that, unlike (for example) Gareth, who from kitchen knave fights his way painfully step by step through the stages of a hard-won initiation, Galahad stands before us from the first with all this already "given", as though already

behind him lay others lives of long spiritual development
– as though he had already achieved a higher form of
consciousness.

Of the spiritual significance of the Arthurian and Grail
stories Rudolf Steiner has given us the following indications:

Those of King Arthur's Round Table hold a repetition
of what the candidate for Initiation had to experience in
the Sentient Soul.

The content of the Grail legends, with the exception of
Parzival, is what can be experienced in modern times
by the Intellectual Soul.

Parzival is a picture placed in Europe in the Fourth
Epoch to prepare for the development of the Consciousness Soul in the Fifth Epoch.

We ask ourselves:

Could the fourth step of this sequence be that Galahad
is a picture placed in the country of the Consciousness
Soul* in the Fifth Epoch to prepare for the development
of Spirit-Self in the Sixth?

In contemplating *Le Morte d'Arthur*, written at the
threshold of our own epoch, one had the strong impression that it looks before and after, pointing on one hand
to the past imaginative consciousness of the epoch of the
Sentient Soul, and on the other to the future imaginative consciousness of the epoch of Spirit-Self. The one
soul-principle is a metamorphosis of the other – Spirit-
Self is Sentient Soul, cleansed, uplifted, sanctified. Such
a metamorphosis was the ultimate goal of the Round
Table's striving. Can we perhaps, in Malory, see this
Sentient Soul striving upwards through manifold stages
and manifestations – through, among others, Kay, Pel-
inore, Bagdemagus, Gawaine, Lancelot, Bors, Percivale
– to flower, in Galahad, in Spirit-Self itself?

* *For this and similar expressions on this page see R. Steiner's "An Outline
of Esoteric Science", Ch. 2.*

Rudolf Steiner tells us that, in the Sixth Epoch, faces will show good and evil, as forms also will in the Seventh. Galahad, at his knighting, was "so passing fair and well-made that unnethe (scarcely) in the world might men find his match. Lancelot beheld the young squire and saw him seemly and demure as a dove, with all manner of good features, so that he deemed of his age never to have seen so fair a man of form."

"God make you a good man," he says to him. "for beauty faileth you not as any that liveth."

"Seemly and demure as a dove." The dove is a picture of the Holy Spirit. At Pentecost, Galahad is knighted; at Pentecost he comes to Camelot, the harbinger of the Grail itself. Again and again this connection is delicately indicated.

It is when Galahad takes his place in the Siege Perilous that Camelot experiences its Grail Pentecost. "All who were present were alighted of the grace of the Holy Ghost. Then began every knight to behold every other, by their seeming, fairer that ever they saw before."

Mordrains, Galahad's ancient ancestor, that "passing old man of three hundred winters," refers quite openly and specifically to Galahad's connection with the Paraclete – "the fire of the Holy Ghost is so taken in thee that my flesh, which was of dead oldness, has become young again."

The last appearance of the Grail at Carbonek is like a seed laid by the archetypal Pentecost into prepared hearts, to await its flowering in an epoch yet to come. The place of the twelve apostles is taken by the twelve knights, the place Christian tradition accords to Mary by King Pelleas' niece; perhaps in the sick king brought in for healing one can see a promise for future humanity.

Of the nine knights who join the "three white bulls,"
three are from Gaul, three from Ireland, three from
Denmark. One is reminded of Rudolf Steiner's prophetic words:
"The stream of Philadelphia will be a small group
drawn from every tribe and nation, surviving into the
next epoch of the war of all against all, striving together
towards the spiritualising of the planet."

Galahad's salutation to the knights at Camelot is a
Manas salutation – "peace be with you, fair lords."
"Man will be more peaceful and harmonious," Rudolf
Steiner has told us, "when Spirit-Self draws into
human beings. The Sixth Epoch will bring peace and
brotherhood."
This brotherhood broods dove-like over Galahad's
words and deeds. Of this King Arthur shows his awareness in his first greeting – "Sir, you be welcome, for you
shall move many good knights unto the Quest of the
Sancgreal" – that is, carry their striving with you. For
the Grail is achieved not for oneself but for humanity.
In the Ship of Solomon, also, when Percival's sister has
set the new girdle about the sword, Bors and Percivale
say to Galahad:
"In the name of Jesu Christ, we pray you that ye gird
you with this sword that hath been so much desired in
the realm of Logres."
But Galahad replies:
"Let me begin to grip this sword, for to give you courage. For wit ye well that it belongeth ne more to me
than it doth to you."
And when, on that last evening at Carbonek, the nine

stranger-knights partake of the Eucharist with them, Galahad asks of Christ:

"Sir, why shall not these other fellows go with us?"

In the epoch following ours, Rudolf Steiner tells us, "men will have to be capable of perceiving the light behind all things, the world of spirit which brings everything in existence." Galahad beheld this light, and, more, the beings of the light. Not only was he aware of the angels who served the Grail, but even his shield was the gift of a supersensible being, who, in the form of a knight in white armour, instructed him in his history and then vanished away. We have even the testimony of fiends that Galahad himself was encompassed by angels.

But transcending this perception of the light and of the beings in the light, Galahad's soul-faculties were transformed into those still higher faculties of the future to which the Christ Himself will be visible in the coming epoch. "In the next three thousand years, Rudolf Steiner tells us, "it will no longer be necessary to have religious teaching or documents. Through actual perception, through actual vision of the Christ, men will themselves be able to understand."

At Carbonek, when King Pelleas and his son had withdrawn, leaving behind only those who were to be fed by the Grail, "there came a man from heaven, clothed in likeness of a bishop, that had a cross in his hands; and four angels bare him in a chair, and set him down

before the table of silver where on the Sancgreal was.
"And it seemed that he had in the middes of his forehead letters the which said:

"'See ye here Joseph, the first bishop of Christendom.'

"Then the knights marvelled, for that bishop was dead
more than three hundred years tofore.

"'O knights,'said he, 'marvel not, for I was sometime an
earthly man.'"

The beings of the light who encompassed Galahad were
not beings of the heavenly hierarchies alone. Malory
records that "many of the knights of the Round Table
were slain and destroyed, more that half." It would be
in harmony with what Anthroposophy can tell us about
the so-called dead that many of these could have carried
over to the other side concern for this renewal of
chivalry on a higher plane. When Malory, reports that,
at the castle of the Dish of Blood. "Galahad fought as if
he were no earthly man," we can reasonably surmise
that he may well have had invisible help, for our
teacher has recorded the following sustaining indication
concerning Spirit-Self:

"We dream in feeling, so do not know that the dead
walk with us. In the Culture now preparing, we shall
have to ask, when making a decision: 'What do the
dead think of it?' In the future we shall know that the
dead are the wisest of counsellors, whom we may con-
sult when we wish to do something of Earth. The
Spirit-Self develops through the fact that the dead are
counsellors of the living.

The language of heraldry expressed a knight's inner
being symbolically in a device of his shield and banner,

and in the crest on his helmet. In one medieval illumination the crest of Galahad's helmet consists of the head
and shoulders of an angel. If it is not a now forgotten
tradition, this crest would seem to suggest a flash of
intuitive understanding of Galahad's stage in evolution
by the medieval artist which it has needed Anthroposophy to indicate in our time. For Anthroposophy
tells us that in the sixth Epoch a man's true highest being
will not be *in* his body but *beside* it.

One's surmise that the artist is aware of the angel as
something more than an inanimate crest is supported
by the fact that Galahad's most pressing opponent –
one of the Seven Deadly Sins of the Castle of Maidens –
is wielding two lances, one aimed at Galahad's brow,
and the other at the heart of the angel.

"In the Persian initiation," we are told, "the fifth
degree was attained by him who had already transformed his soul, the Daëna, into Spirit-Self. He had
thus become bearer of a higher Spirit-being, a Yazata or
Archangel. This archangel represents the Folk-Soul.
This degree of initiation is therefore designated by the
name of the folk."

The Greek Orthodox Church is the vessel of that form
of Christianity which until our times has nourished
those parts of Europe in which Philadelphia will have
its home. Its ritual still retains an invocation to the
Holy Spirit now missing in most of the Christian rituals
of the West. Its altar is invisible behind a screen, the
iconastasis; but for congregation standing outside it
this "wall of pictures" portrays the spiritual realities
being enacted within. For Galahad Transubstantiation

was not a dogma but an experience; Russian ikons sub-
limely portray the supersensible mystery described by
Malory when Joseph of Arimathea, for the last time at
Carbonek, "goes to the sacring of the mass":
"Then he took an ubbly (wafer) which was made in
likeness of bread. And at the lifting up there came a
figure in likeness of a child, and smote himself into the
bread. Then he put it into the holy vessel again, and did
what it belonged to a priest to do at a mass. And when
he had done this, he vanished away.
"Then looked they and saw a man come out of the holy
vessel, that had all the signs of the Passion of Jesu
Christ, bleeding all openly."
And Christ Himself administered the Sacrament to
them.

"A man that had all the signs of the Passion, bleeding
all openly."
We know from the Gospels that Christ's Resurrection
body bore the marks of the five wounds – "Then saith
He to Thomas, Reach hither thy finger, and behold My
hands; and reach hither thy hand, and thrust it into My
side."
Rudolf Steiner tells us that the fourth stage of the
mediaeval Christian Initiation was the Crucifixion.
"When a man's body has become external to him, so
that he bears it in and out of the doorway as something
external, not himself, there is revealed to him what is
called 'the Ordeal of the Blood.' Certain reddenings of
the skin appear in such a way that he can call forth the
wounds of Christ, on the hands, the feet, and on the
right side of the breast. When the pupils, by the depth of

feeling, is able to develop in himself the Blood Ordeal, the external symptom, then there appears likewise the inner, the astral, in which he sees himself crucified."

The Five Wounds are dwelt on with awe and compassion in mediaeval poems, as in this one from a manuscript in Durham cathedral (1225-50 A.D.):

> "White was His naked breast,
>   And red of blood His side;
> Pale was His fair face,
> His wounds deep and wide,
>
> And His arms y-straight,
>   High upon the rood;
> From five places of His body,
>   The streams ran of blood."

The Five Wounds were remembered in the five grains of incense placed in the Paschal candle, in the five relics placed in cavities in the new altar at its consecration, and in the crosses adorned with five jewels portrayed in early mosaics. That this last commemoration went back to Anglo-Saxon times is shown in *The Dream of the Rood*:

> "Hwaet!*
> It seemed I saw the Tree itself
> Borne on the air, light wound about it,
> A beam of brightest wood, a beacon-cloud
> In overlapping god, with glancing gems
> Fair at its foot.
> Five stones set in a crux
> Flashed from the cross-tree."

In the *Grand Saint Graal*, attributed to Walter Map, Archdeacon of Oxford and Chaplain to Henry II, Joseph is divinely directed to build an Ark at Sarras, in

* *Harken!*

which the Grail is to be housed.When he opens the
door of the Ark, he sees the figure of a man within,
clothed in scarlet flame and bleeding from five wounds,
and about him five angels also clothed in flame, each
with six wings of flame, and all bearing the symbols of
the Passion – nails, pincers, scourge – as these are
depicted on Breton menhirs.

This rich imagination becomes transparent in the light
of Rudolf Steiner's indication:

"The Fifth Principle – the beginning of the development
of Manas in humanity – was under the guardianship of
the two Cherubim hovering over the Ark of the Covenant.

"The inside is adorned with gold, symbol of truth. Wisdom now enters into the stage of Manas. We find
palm-leaves as the symbol of peace. This represents a
certain epoch of mankind."

"When the fifth principle comes down from above," we
are told, "out of the square of physical, etheric, astral,
lower ego, a pentagon is made." What seeds of occult
truth lie in this apparently simple and obvious
mathematical statement! For the pentagon encloses the
pentagram –the five-pointed star which is both the star
of Mercury and the basis of the rose.

Dr. Zeylmans von Emmichoven has pointed out how
"the eurhythmist who forms the pentagram does not
move around the outside of the form (as with the hexag-
ram) but remains within the form, *builds it from within*."
We see in the pentagram a picture of the body perme-
ated by the ego.

This completely ego-permeated body Dr. Steiner connects with the five wounds:

"Because the complete ego, in all its strength, had
entered into the body of Christ Jesus, His body had to

receive *five* wounds, not one only.* ... How would a body be seen if the full power of the ego had entered it? It would be seen with five wounds."

Russia's present soul-condition can place a certain stumbling-block in one's ready acceptance of Steiner's indication of her destined part in the next stage of evolution, as when he says:

"It lives in the nature of the Russian people that what can only take place in the rest of Europe in a preliminary stage can come into the world with instinctive power, with elemental force, with historic necessity, through Russianism. To the Russian people as a nation is given the mission of building up the Grail-system as a religious system until the Sixth Post-Atlanean epoch, so that it can then become the ferment of cultures of the whole earth."

But then he gently leads us by the hand towards a wider outlook:

"'Christ is Spirit' is something extremely intimate, something that belongs to the noblest culture of the Consciousness Soul; and now it came up [i.e. in modern Russia] in what is living in the Sentient Soul, where socialism rumbles. No wonder that the spread of socialism in these Eastern parts of Europe takes forms that are inconceivable to the rest of the world, an unorganised interplay of the Consciousness Soul culture and Sentient Soul culture.

"If these inward connections are grasped, much that happens in external reality will become clear and comprehensible. And it is already necessary for present-day humanity and its future evolution that it should not

---

* As with Sigurd and Achilles

pass by the relationships of the time in which we now
stand. Hitherto it had not been understood; that is why
the European chaos came about."

And, as always, he does not leave us destitute of
building-stones:

"Each epoch has, on the one hand, to cultivate a particular form of culture and of spiritual life primarily
concerned with the external and visible world. But each
epoch must at the same time prepare, bear within it at a
preparatory stage, what is to come in the ensuing period
of culture.

"Our task in Spiritual Science is not only to acquire
spiritual treasure for ourselves, for the eternal life of the
soul but also to prepare what will constitute the content, the specific external work, of the Sixth Culture
Epoch.

"The work achieved on Earth by intimate assemblies
connected with the Mysteries in each epoch has been of
such a nature that forces flowed upwards to the Spirits
of the Higher Hierarchies, enabling them to nourish
and cultivate what was to stream down into the souls of
men in a later epoch.

By uniting in brotherliness in working groups, something hovers invisibly over our work, something that is
like the child of the forces of the Spirit-Self."

In *Perceval li Gallois*, Gawaine says of Perceval:
"All of knighthood that may be lodged in the body is in
him."

But with Galahad it hovers around and above him, as
Spirit-Self will do in the Sixth Epoch. Thus others, too,
may be drawn into its circle.

Parzival's is the lonelier path of an earlier epoch; but it is Galahad's mission to take others with him, to destroy evil customs, to deliver souls from thrall. One receives the impression that his healing of the cripple immediately the Ship of Solomon touches land at Sarras is an archetypal gesture, born of Spirit-Self:

"Then they took out of the ship the table of silver, and Pecivale and Bors took it to go tofore, and Galahad came behind. And right so they went to the city, and at the gate of the city they saw an old man, crooked.

"Then Galahad called to him and bade him help to bear this heavy thing.

"'Truly,' said the old man, 'it is ten years ago that I might not go but with crutches.'

"'Care thou not,' said Galahad. 'But arise up and shew thy good will.'

"And so he essayed, and found himself as whole as ever he was. Then ran he to the table and took one part against Galahad. And anon arose there great noises in the city, that a cripple was made whole by knights marvellous that entered into the city."

Galahad does indeed work all by miracle, for he works out of the forces of the future. In Malory Lancelot says of the dead Elaine:

"Well I wot that she bore the best knight that is on the earth, *or that ever was since God was born.*"

"The last phase of Christianity," says Rudolf Steiner, "which was inaugurated by the Initiate Lohengrin, introduced the period of utilitarianism which has now reached its peak. Even the materialism of modern times owes its origin to great Initiates; for it is always Initiates who speak when a new impulse is to be given to civilisation. But materialism must be superseded by a new phase, a new cycle. It is this new phase that

Anthroposophy seeks to introduce." Elsewhere he gath-
ers all these indications into one clarion-call:
"Anthroposophy is the new search for the Grail."

"Thus endeth
The story of the Sangreal,
the which is a story
chronicled for one of the truest and the holiest
that is in the world."
Malory

REFERENCES

St.John XX, 27.
The Foundation Stone, F.W. Zeylmans van
Emmichoven, (R. Steiner Press).

LECTURES by RUDOLF STEINER:

The Mysteries of the East and of Christianity,
  Berlin, 3-7 Feb. 1913.

The Apocalypse of St. John,
  Nuremberg, 17-30 June 1908.

Jeschu ben Pandira, A Herald of the Christ Impulse,
  Dornach, 4, 5 Nov. 1911. See in "Esoteric Christianity".

Rosicrucian Christianity,
  Neuchatel, 28 Sept. 1911. See in "Esoteric Christianity".

Rosicrucian Wisdom,
  Munich, 22 May-6 June 1907.

The Gospel of St. Mark,
  Basle, 15-24 Sept. 1912.

Old and New Methods of Initiation,
  Dornach, 8 Jan. 1922, (R. Steiner Press).

Preparing for the 6th Epoch, see also *The Reverse Ritual*,
  Dusseldorf, 15 June 1915, (Anthroposophic Press).

Parsifal and Lohengrin,
  Cologne, 3 Dec. 1905. See Z 212.

COMPLETE LIST OF REFERENCES

(1) *Anglo-Saxon Chronicle*, London
(2) Aubert, Louis: *Légendes Traditionelles de la Bretagne*
(3) Benning, M.C.: *Merlin und König Artus*, Stuttgart, 1980
(4) Holy Bible
(5) *Black Letter Gospel of Nicodemus*, 1511, printed by Wynkin de Worde (British Museum, London)
(6) Chaucer: *Canterbury Tales*, Penguin Books
(7) Chrètien de Troyes: *Erec and Enid* in *Arthurian Romances*, Dent: Everyman
(8) Chrètien de Troyes: *Gauwain sucht den Gral*, Stuttgart, 1986
(9) Chrètien de Troyes: *Perceval*, Continuations, D.S. Brewer
(10) Chrètien de Troyes: *Lancelot* in *Arthurian Romances*, Dent: Everyman.
(11) Chrètien de Troyes: *Perceval der Gralskönig*, Stuttgart, 1983
(12) Chrètien de Troyes: *Perceval* in *Arthurian Romances*, Dent: Everyman
(13) Konrad Fleck: *Flore and Blanchefleur*, St. George Publications, 1977.
(15) *Gospel of Nicodemus* – see *Apocryphal New Testament*; Translation M.R. James, Oxford Univ. Press
(16) *Jack the Giant Killer* – see Joseph Jacobs: *English Fairy Tales*, Dent: Everyman
(17) Josephus: *Antiquities of the Jews*, Loab Classical Library
(18) Layamon – See 73
(19) *Legendes Traditionelles de la Bretagne*
(20) Loomis, R.S.: *Arthurian Literature in the Middle Ages*
(21) *Mabinogion*, Penguin Books
(22) Thomas Malory: *Le Morte d'Arthur*, Oxford Univ. Press
(23) Meyer, Rudolf: *Der Gral und seine Hüter*
(24) *New Testament*, translated Emil Bock, Stuttgart 1989
(25) Ordinalia: 14 Jh.
(26) *Perceval li Gallois* – see *The High Book of the Grail*, D.S. Brewer
(27) Robert de Boron: *Petit Saint Graal*
(28) *The Presely Hills*, Pembrokeshire National Park Publications
(29) *Prophecies of Merlin*, Edited by R.J. Stewart, Arkana

(30) *The Quest of the Holy Grail*, Harmondsworth 1982

(31) Roach, W: *Notes to the Didot Perceval*

(32-34) Robert de Boron: *Merlin and the Grail*, D.S. Brewer

(35) W.J. Stein: *The Ninth Century*, Temple Lodge

(36) Steiner, Rudolf: *Old and New Methods of Initiation*, (GA 210),
     R. Steiner Press, 1991

(37) Steiner, Rudolf: *The Apocalypse of St. John*, (GA 104),
     R. Steiner Press, 1977

(38) Steiner, Rudolf: *Christ and the Spiritual World*, (GA 149),
     R. Steiner Press, 1963

(39) Steiner, Rudolf: *Richard Wagner und die Mystik*, (GA 55),
     R. Steiner Press, 1997

(40) Steiner, Rudolf: *Karmic Relationships, Vol. 4*, (GA 238),
     Dornach, 1983

(41) Steiner, Rudolf: *Karmic Relationships, Vol. 6*, (GA 240),
     R. Steiner Press, 1971

(42) Steiner, Rudolf: *Esoteric Christianity*, (GA 130),
     R. Steiner Press, 2000

(43) Steiner, Rudolf: see No. 42

(44) Steiner, Rudolf: see No. 42

(45) Steiner, Rudolf: *Background to the Gospel of St. Mark*, (GA 124),
     R. Steiner Press, 1968

(46) Steiner, Rudolf: GA 159/60 (only partly translated)

(47) Steiner, Rudolf: *The Mystery of the Trinity*, (GA 214),
     Anthroposophic Press, 1991

(48) Steiner, Rudolf: *The Principle of Spiritual Economy*, (GA 109/111),
     RSP/AP 1986

(49) Steiner, Rudolf: *History of the Middle Ages*, (GA 51),
     typescript R 88/89

(50) Steiner, Rudolf: *From Symptom to Reality in Modern History*,
     (GA 185), RSP 1976

(51) Steiner, Rudolf: *Supersensible Influences in the History of Mankind*,
     (GA 216), Anth. Publ. Co., 1956

(52) Steiner, Rudolf: *The Gospel of John & its Relation to the Other
     Gospels*, (GA 112), AP 1982

(53) Steiner, Rudolf: *The Gospel of St. Mark*, (GA 139), P/RSP 1986

(54) Steiner, Rudolf: GA 61, only partly translated

(55) Steiner, Rudolf: *The Mysteries of the East and of Christianity*, (GA 144), RSP 1972

(56) Steiner, Rudolf: *The East in the Light of the West*, (GA 113), Blauvelt, 1986

(57) Steiner, Rudolf: *Parsifal*: Berlin 19.5.1905, typescript NSL 175-8; Landin 29.7.1906, *The Christian Mystery*, (GA 97), Completion Press, 2000

(58) Steiner, Rudolf: *Materialism and the Task of Anthroposophy*, (GA 204), AP/RSP 1987

(59) Steiner, Rudolf: *The Principle of Spiritual Economy*, (GA 109), RSP/AP 1986

(60) Steiner, Rudolf: *Richard Wagner*, typescript NSL 175-8

(61) Steiner, Rudolf: *The Temple Legend*, (GA 93), RSP 1985

(62) Steiner, Rudolf: *Rosicrucian Wisdom/Theosophy of the Rosicrucians*, (GA 99), RSP 2000

(63) Steiner, Rudolf: *The Work of the Angels in Man's Astral Body*, see also in *Angels,* RSP 1996

(64) Steiner, Rudolf: *Zeichen der Zeit 1918*, (GA 182), Dornach, 1976

(65) Steiner, Rudolf: *White Magic Contrasted with Black*, Typescript Z 306

(66) Steiner, Rudolf: *Parzival und Lohengrin*, (GA 54), Dornach 1963. see also in *Angels,* RSP 1996

(67) Steiner, Rudolf: *Toward Imagination*, (GA 169), AP 1990

(68) Steiner, Rudolf: *The European Mysteries and the Initiates*, Anthroposophical Quarterly, Vol. 9, No. 1

(69) Thomas à Kempis: *The Imitation of Christ,* Penguin Books

(70) Tolland: *History of the Druids*

(71) Tomberg, Valentin: *Studies in the Old Testament*

(72) Geoffrey of Monmouth: *The Life of Merlin*, University of Wales Press, 1973

(73) Wace and Layamon: *Roman de Brut – Arthurian Chronicles*, London 1977

(74) Williams, Charles: *Taliesin thrugh Logres (The Last Voyage)*

(75) Wolfram von Eschenbach: *Parzival*, Penguin Books

(76) Woodmartin: *Trace of the Elder Faiths of Ireland*

(77) F.W. Zeylmans van Emmichoven: *The Foundation Stone*, Temple Lodge 2002

REFERENCES in the order in which they have been used by the author.

Ch. I   – 21, 6, 10, 73, 26, 40, 51 9, 41.
Ch. II   – 21, 7, 41, 44.
Ch. III   – 40, 51, 41, 58, 67.
Ch. IV   – 26, 22, 5, 32, 15, 69, 52.
Ch. V   – 61, 52.
Ch. VI   – 14.
Ch. VII   – 4, 17, 65, 71, 75, 57.
Ch. VIII – 13, 59, 75, 35, 61, 48, 49, 60, 66, 68.
Ch. IX   – 32, 33, 4, 26, 32, 56, 22.
Ch. X   – 73, 54, 72, 28, 4, 33, 56, 43, 47.
Ch. XI   – 29, 19, 76, 34, 70, 7, 31, 20, 60.
Ch. XII   – 10, 22, 37, 42, 64, 77, 53, 50, 22, 46, 36, 55, 63.